Put It in Writing!

Put It in Writing!

Creating Agreements Between Family and Friends

Deborah Hutchison and
Lynn Toler, Judge of *Divorce Court*

STERLING

New York / London
www.sterlingpublishing.com

To Madge,
because I miss you

—D. H.

To my father,

William A. Toler

—L. T.

STERLING and the distinctive Sterling logo are registered trademarks of Sterling Publishing Co., Inc.

LIBRARY OF CONGRESS CATALOGING-IN-PUBLICATION DATA

Hutchison, Deborah.
  Put it in writing! : creating agreements between family and friends / by Deborah Hutchison and Lynn Toler.
    p. cm.
  Includes index.
  ISBN 978-1-4027-5870-6 (pb-trade pbk. : alk. paper) 1. Contracts—United States—Popular works. 2. Parent and child (Law)—United States—Popular works. 3. Domestic relations—United States—Popular works. 4. Interpersonal relations—United States—Popular works. I. Toler, Lynn. II. Title.
  KF801.Z9H88 2009
  346.7302—dc22

                                                                2009005588

10 9 8 7 6 5 4 3 2 1

Published by Sterling Publishing Co., Inc.
387 Park Avenue South, New York, NY 10016
Text © 2009 by Deborah Hutchison and Lynn Toler
Agreements © Panther Productions, Inc.
Sane Approach to an Emotional Issue™ Panther Productions, Inc.

Distributed in Canada by Sterling Publishing
c/o Canadian Manda Group, 165 Dufferin Street
Toronto, Ontario, Canada M6K 3H6
Distributed in the United Kingdom by GMC Distribution Services
Castle Place, 166 High Street, Lewes, East Sussex, England BN7 1XU
Distributed in Australia by Capricorn Link (Australia) Pty. Ltd.
P.O. Box 704, Windsor, NSW 2756, Australia

Book design by Richard Oriolo

Manufactured in the United States of America
All rights reserved

Sterling ISBN 978-1-4027-5870-6

For information about custom editions, special sales, premium and corporate purchases, please contact Sterling Special Sales Department at 800-805-5489 or specialsales@sterlingpublishing.com.

CONTENTS

Acknowledgments   vii

A Note from the Authors   viii

Introduction: There Must Be a Better Way, by Deborah Hutchison   1

Part I: Taking the Sane Approach   5

Chapter 1   It Takes Two   7

Chapter 2   Writing It Down   11
                Filling in the Blanks   12
                Before You Sign   17
                After You Sign   17

Chapter 3   How to Enforce Your Agreement   19
                The Easy Way   20
                Formal Dispute Resolution   21
                Small Claims Court   22

Part II: The Most Common Situations and Agreements   25

Chapter 4   Brother, Can You Spare a Dime?   27
                The Lending Money Agreement

Chapter 5   It Isn't Mine to Keep?   39
                The Lending Personal Property Agreement

Chapter 6   They're Back!   49
                The Temporary Residence/Grown Child Returns Home Agreement

Chapter 7   For the Sake of the Children   63
                The Shared Parenting for Separated/Divorced Parents Agreement

Chapter 8   Siblings Unite!   77
                The Caring for Our Aging Parents Agreement

Chapter 9   Mom, Can I Have the Keys?   91
                The Safe Driving Parent–Teen Driver Agreement

Chapter 10   Move Over, Rover!   103
                      The Shared Pet/Pet Parenting Agreement

Chapter 11   My Home Is Your Home   115
                      The Lending Your Vacation Home Agreement

Chapter 12   Just Between Us   127
                      The Personal Confidentiality Agreement

Chapter 13   Where Is Your Rent Check?   135
                      The Roommate Agreement

Chapter 14   Do It Yourself   151
                      Blank Agreement for Any Arrangement

Index   161

Agreements Index   164

ACKNOWLEDGMENTS

Creating this book has been an incredible journey, and without the support and encouragement of many people it could never have happened. I thank Angela Rinaldi, my wonderful agent, for the book deal with Sterling Publishing.

I owe tremendous gratitude to mediator Deanie Kramer, who introduced me to "Judge Lynn" Toler of *Divorce Court,* the coauthor of this book. Lynn Toler is one absolutely amazing woman. From the moment we were introduced, I felt the camaraderie. It was a pleasure to work alongside such a professional, one who is also so giving, so honest, and a person who could laugh when we needed to. Lynn, you are a wonderful collaborator and an ideal coauthor!

This book could not have been completed without the much-appreciated help of Patricia Medved, who was always there with a word, a sentence, and a paragraph. Accumulating research material and organizing and working on the agreements was a big undertaking. Therese Cummings, Caitlin Berry, Shannon Brown, Meg Richard, and Brittany Votto—I'm thankful for your help, time, and participation.

Meredith Hale from Sterling Publishing, you became our editor after we started with Jo Fagan (thanks for the start, Jo), and it's been a pleasure to work with you.

Lois Phillips, your suggestion to put the agreements in a book started this entire process, and it's been an amazing ride. Dawn Willson, you helped jump-start this book, and here it is. Helen Arnold, a very special thanks for your help as an advisor and, most important, as a good friend. You always bring clarity to any situation. Jane Heller, nothing like a pro to help a newbie in the book world—not only did I appreciate your words of wisdom, but I could not wait to read your books when I needed an escape.

Judy Swope, we created the agreement for your family of kids when they were moving back home from college. Today not only are kids moving home, parents are moving into their children's homes.

A big thanks goes out to my circle of friends who have always been there for me.

Many thanks to all the people who kindly shared their stories for this book.

To my family and friends, with whom I use the agreements (sister Liz, brother Bill, friend Dawn, interns Brittany, Meg, and Carina, Shannon, Patricia, and my coauthor Lynn), by signing we have created clarity and documentation.

Last, but most important, I have immense love and gratitude for Hall, my wonderfully supportive husband, who has never wavered in his belief in my dreams and who has never counted the hours that he himself has put into them.

—D. H.

I would like to thank my husband, Eric. He's always on board for whatever I do and he holds me up. I, too, would like to thank Deanie Kramer for introducing me to Deborah. What a pleasure it has been. I would also like to thank Deserie Davenport, who helps me keep my professional and domestic lives stitched together. She says things like "I've got you covered" and "Girl, I know how you feel."

—L. T.

A NOTE FROM THE AUTHORS

This book does not constitute legal advice. We believe that writing things down and using these written agreements can be a helpful process. The agreements were designed to be simple and clear. We did not intend them to be as comprehensive as a formal contract would be. These are meant to be used between family members and friends who have a vested interest in preserving their relationships.

The agreements are tools for better, more reliable, and productive communication between two or more people. Still, misunderstandings can crop up. You may decide that you need an attorney to help sort matters out or to pursue a situation beyond the scope of the agreement.

These agreements are not a substitute for legal advice. If you are interested in drafting a contract to protect your legal interests, you should consult an attorney. A lawyer will be experienced, and will understand the laws of your state and how they may apply to your specific situation.

Keep in mind that anything in writing could serve as proof of an agreement in court, but we are not making any representations about their legal use here. By using these agreements, you agree that the authors, publisher, and seller shall not be liable for any damages of any kind, including special, incidental, or consequential damages.

Introduction:
There Must Be a Better Way

by Deborah Hutchison

The first time I truly realized the value of putting something in writing was after my divorce. The court had ordered my ex to pay me back for supporting him during medical school, but he didn't pay. I was frustrated and angry. I could have pursued this through expensive legal channels, but my lawyer needed proof that I was trying to collect. My ex didn't return my phone calls and never answered my letters, so I wanted a quicker, cleaner solution. I decided to send him an actual bill in the mail each month. This worked! Having documentation in hand was enough to keep him on track with his payments. I was so encouraged by my success, I created a billing system—*Bill Your Ex*—so that women and men everywhere could use the same technique.

When empty-nester friends of mine had three adult children moving back home at the same time, I suggested that they write up an agreement so that there would be no misunderstandings. Together we drafted the Temporary Residence Agreement. One child was happy to have clear parameters, one was indifferent, and the third was reluctant to sign. Yet they all signed eventually, and helped to make what could have been a volatile living situation into a smooth transition time for themselves and their parents. As a true testament to the value of the Temporary Residence Agreement, all three children are now out on their own and doing quite well. Thus was born the A Sane Approach to an Emotional Issue™ concept.

I've had occasion to lend friends money and, in the past, I have been taken advantage of. In one case, I lost my money and my friend. Then I decided to try writing an agreement before lending a friend any money. This became the Lend Money to Friends and Family Agreement—my second A Sane Approach to an Emotional Issue agreement. In it I spelled out a payment plan. Emotionally, I felt inner peace. I was happy to lend and felt protected at the same time.

What I have discovered is that writing up an agreement helps everyone involved move past the emotions that come up when we deal with friends and family members. Agreements make it possible to help each other and at the same time establish boundaries so that relationships aren't put in jeopardy by miscommunication or misunderstandings. Here's another example:

Several years ago, my husband's mother gave him a large painting, which we did not have room to hang in our house. His brother had just bought a house with lots of wall space. We thought we could offer the painting to him to store on his wall until we needed it. Apparently, we weren't clear that it was a loan, because when we wanted it back, my husband's brother did not want to return it. It had become part of his décor. Uh-oh. We were totally surprised. He thought we had given it to him. After we communicated our original intention, he did return the painting, but the experience prompted me to create this book.

You've probably found yourself in similar situations. Have you ever lent money to a friend, only to find yourself out $50, $500, or $5,000—and the friendship? Have you ever agreed to let a family member live under your roof temporarily, only to find yourself frustrated and cramped, with no relief in sight? Have you ever argued with a roommate over who gets to keep the dog you shared because you love the dog but can no longer stand each other?

If it hasn't happened to you, you probably have friends who've experienced a situation like one of these. When people are let down by those close to them, the emotional fallout can be considerable. After all, a trust has been breached and, most of the time, there is no record of what has transpired. If the parties are still speaking at all, their conversations have probably eroded into *"he said . . ."/"she said . . ."* And it isn't long before the ill will begins to infect everyone around them.

I wrote this book because I want to show people that there is a better way—what I call the Sane Approach. Taking the Sane Approach simply means putting the terms of an arrangement or agreement in writing. Consider it a professional approach to dealing with personal situations. Yes, you can do this even with family members and close friends. *Especially* with family members and close friends. When it comes to family and close friends, a written agreement can mean the difference between seeing your money again as opposed to kissing it good-bye, helping your child get on her feet as opposed to playing perpetual hostess to a slacker, sharing the companionship of a pet as opposed to sending it back to the shelter, and, most important, building a stronger bond as opposed to fracturing a relationship.

When my friend's sister was buying her first house, she knew her credit check would turn up some bad debt. She asked my friend if she could borrow money to pay off her credit cards so she would be approved for her mortgage. That made sense, and my friend wanted to help. But my friend never asked how her sister would pay her back once she took on monthly mortgage payments—and she was still maintaining the bad habits that had caused her to rack up debt in the first place. My friend's sister is working hard to make ends meet and my friend doesn't want to hold the money her sister owes her over her head, but she never intended to just give the money to her. Now my friend wishes she had written down that her sister would pay her back someday, even if it wasn't until she sold the house!

Too often, we enter into emotionally loaded situations with nothing more than a promise or maybe a handshake between us. Sometimes we skip even that. This leaves both parties vulnerable to misunderstanding. Consider the family quarrels and broken friendships you've encountered. Chances are that miscommunication and confusion about money or responsibility were at the heart of the problem. And we've seen that it doesn't take long for a simple misunderstanding to blossom into an irreparable feud.

Written agreements signed by both parties are far superior to oral and implied agreements, because they give the parties some certainty and clarity. They help everyone by establishing, upfront, the exact terms of their understanding. They become tools for better communication.

The key reason *Put It in Writing!* works so well is that it respects the points of view and the needs of both parties. The process encourages participants to think through potential problems and to agree to ground rules that will help avoid problems down the road. The agreements also serve as evidence of both parties' commitment and desire to make the situation work. Written agreements offer peace of mind and set us up for the elusive win-win situation. They can make it easy to help out the people we care about or to ask for help when we really need it.

We live in a cautious society. We sign agreements all the time: when we read something on an Internet site, when our children join the soccer team, when we subscribe to the newspaper, when we buy a new TV. But often, with the people closest to us, we fail to take this simple step and we put our relationships in jeopardy. In this book, we provide guidelines for writing agreements to cover almost any situation, so there is no excuse for leaving things to good faith (which too often goes bad!).

Below is another story from a friend:

After graduating from college, Tonya's son found a job in the media. It paid next to nothing, but he was pursuing his dream and Tonya was proud of that. He couldn't afford to rent his own place, so he moved back home. Then the trouble started. He would "work" late nearly every night, crash, and then leave again early the next morning. On weekends, he partied and slept in. Tonya's younger son was picking up on this behavior and she didn't feel it should be going on in her home. When Tonya finally tried to discuss it with her son, he accused her of failing to be supportive. Meanwhile, she felt that all she was doing was being supportive! Things definitely got worse before he finally moved out. An agreement ahead of time would have saved this family a lot of grief.

We certainly understand that there are some obstacles to our "no-brainer" approach. It's hard telling someone to whom you are close, "I love you, I trust you, but I want a written agreement." The other party may get insulted and upset. The commonsense guidelines in this book can help you take the sting out of asking for a written agreement. We will show you how to approach the other party and explain to her how writing things down benefits everyone involved. If approached properly, everyone will see that putting things in writing is a gesture of commitment to a continuing and positive relationship.

Another sticky point to our Sane Approach is keeping your written agreement in force. Even when things are written down, people may forget the specifics or become lazy or sloppy. They may let a payment slip or overlook a violation or two. While this is natural and understandable among friends and family, don't underestimate the importance of upholding the terms you took such care in recording.

If one party fulfills his obligations to the letter while the other disregards the terms entirely, difficulties will arise. We understand that this may happen and address what you should do about it in chapter 3.

I asked Lynn Toler to join me in writing this book. She is a former Municipal Court judge whose jurisdiction included small claims actions. She saw, firsthand, all the madness and the sadness that arises among family and friends when there is an agreement without documentation. Judge Lynn, as she is called on her nationally syndicated television show *Divorce Court,* has seen the worst cases of *he said/she said* in Small Claims Court, much of which could have been avoided if someone had pulled out a pen and paper and written something down.

Together we created this book to show you how to use the agreements we've included and how to write your own simple agreement to make your life less stressful.

We know how hard it can be to ask someone you care for to enter into a written agreement. Even if you manage to do so, choosing the right words and the exact information to include can be tough. We have created simple agreements that will assist you in common, yet uncomfortable situations that often arise between family and friends. We have addressed not only the *what* and the *why,* but also the difficult question of *how.*

So, the next time someone wants to borrow money, or perhaps you need to borrow money, *put it in writing;* the next time someone wants your ideas or you want to share ideas, *put it in writing;* when your teen passes the road test and asks to use your car, *put it in writing;* if you lend your brother a painting to store temporarily, *put it in writing;* should you decide to share a dwelling with others, set the parameters and *put them in writing.* There are all kinds of situations that call for written documentation of some kind. Once you start to write things down, you'll see that *Put It in Writing* can become a valuable tool in your daily life.

PART I

Taking the Sane Approach

CHAPTER 1

It Takes Two

Family and friends. That's who people turn to first when they need help, and that's the way it should be. Unfortunately, we have all heard horror stories about close relationships torn apart because of misunderstandings about money, property, or responsibility. Neither blood nor friendship can simplify a complicated arrangement. Good intentions won't clarify misunderstandings. Written agreements can, however, help with all these things.

Helping someone close to you can be an incredibly rewarding experience if you approach it correctly. If you set boundaries, explain your needs, and clarify what you expect, you can help or be helped by those you love and still maintain your relationship.

The first thing a written agreement will do is make you consider the consequences of your decision. By asking someone to put an agreement on paper, you will find out how committed he or she is to living up to promises being made. In addition, considering a written agreement will make you think a few things through that will help you determine whether you are truly comfortable getting involved. Can you really do all the things the agreement promises, such as make a monthly loan payment or have your aging parents live with you for several weeks? Can the person you are entering into it with do the same? Do you have long-standing communication problems with that person? Do you feel uneasy going forward? Remember, you are under no obligation to help someone. Be wise and trust your heart.

Roy and his fiancée, Marta, were planning a honeymoon to the Caribbean. They knew that Roy's Aunt Liz and Uncle John had a house on the beach in St. Maarten. Roy asked his Uncle John if they could use the beach house. His uncle said he would think about it. John and Liz would love to let the newlyweds use the house as a wedding gift, but John couldn't forget that only a few years earlier Roy and his buddies had trashed his mom's house during a party. John wondered if Roy could be trusted now that he was more grown up and about to get married.

If a person does not want to put his intentions in writing, this should raise a red flag. The other party's reluctance could be a sign that he doesn't really mean what he says. If you believe that that is the case, you should say no without guilt. Be supportive yet firm. Try something like this: "I am so sorry. I wish I could help, but I can't. It's just not possible." You do not need to explain why someone else can't have your money or live in your house. If you feel bad, you can ask if there is something else you might be able to do. But whatever you do, don't say yes to something you know won't work for you.

If, however, you have considered all these factors and decide that you want to go forward, there are a number of things you can do to ease the way. First, you have to get the other party to understand why you want the agreement in writing. Your tone of voice and body language are as important as the specific words you use. Smile if you can. Speak lightly and pleasantly. Don't wag your finger or stand back with your arms crossed. You need to keep the exchange positive and focused on the outcome while you discuss the possible obstacles.

Second, you need to listen. Don't be so focused on what you want that you don't pay attention to what the other party is saying. While this all seems logical, don't underestimate the emotions that inevitably come into play. Sometimes the other person may become upset that you asked to put things in writing. If that is the case, a little assurance should clear up that concern. Tell him that it is not a matter of trust but a simple effort to avoid misunderstanding by keeping a record. Remind him of the stories you've heard of mutual friends whose relationship with a friend or family member has been irreparably damaged over an arrangement gone bad. Let him read the introductory chapter of this book.

Some phrases you may find useful to include in your conversation:

- "If you want my help, you will have to help me so that we are totally clear. There is no way we want to jeopardize our relationship."

- "How can we make this a win-win situation?"

- "We must work out the details so that both of us are comfortable with the situation."

- "This can benefit both of us."

- "How can we accomplish this without any hard feelings?"

- "I have a terrible time remembering details. Let's write all this down."

- "This way we won't have to discuss things again and again."

- "If anything were to happen, it would be good to have a record."

If someone is asking to borrow money, you are entitled to know what the money is for, but you should be sensitive in the way you ask about this. Give the other party the opportunity to explain her needs. Actively listen to what she has to say so you can respond accordingly. You might say something like this: "I am happy to be in a position to help you with your problem, but I must be totally clear with you so that both of us understand what our agreement will be." Try not to put too many conditions on your offer of assistance, since this may create resentment. However, you should ask enough questions to ensure your own comfort.

If you are the person asking for help, offering to put your promises in writing tells the other party that you will stand by your word. The person you are asking will be more likely to help you when you approach things professionally. He may tell you that he will help you without an agreement. Insist on it anyway. The agreement will protect you both down the road. Misunderstandings can crop up no matter how close two people are.

Once you have decided that you want to enter into a written agreement, you need to make sure both parties understand what the other one needs and wants. You can't have a successful agreement if each side has drastically different expectations. The best way to be sure you understand each other is to parrot the other party. You can say, "Do I understand you correctly? You need X for X period of time and are willing to pay it back by paying X dollars per week, and if you do not comply with your promise, there will be X consequences?" Or, "You would like to use the family car on weekends if you keep your grades up?" You may have to go through this procedure more than once to ensure that you are in agreement.

During this process, you should keep in mind that some people may appreciate having every last detail spelled out while some may find that too restrictive and unnecessary. You will need to feel out the other person and you will want to be comfortable yourself. Sometimes family and close friends feel threatened or vulnerable when you push them to commit to too much on paper. They may withdraw if they feel you are being too rigid or formal. Respect their feelings but go with your gut. While we feel strongly that it is best to have as much in writing as you can, you might have to accept less if you really do trust the other person and don't want to offend. This is something only you will know.

When Sam lost his job and needed to move back into his parents' home, his parents drafted an agreement stipulating all of the conditions they were putting on his return home, including that he needed to find a job and move out within three months. They were trying to keep Sam motivated, but instead it made him feel like a total deadbeat. Didn't his parents know how hard things were? After a heart-to-heart, his parents decided to redraft the agreement without so many stipulations. They could see that Sam was already feeling down and they realized they didn't really want to turn him out on the street if he didn't find a job right away. A more general agreement could achieve their purpose of establishing parameters without insulting their son, who was already having a crisis of confidence.

You have established that you are in agreement and are ready to write things down. Now you can work out the specific details of your arrangement. The next chapter will help you do that.

CHAPTER 2

Writing It Down

Now that you have decided to put your agreement in writing, you are ready to draw up your document. You want to make sure it is written clearly and contains all the details that you need. All agreements should include the full names of the participants, the date the agreement was made, the specific terms you decide to include, and all parties' signatures. There is no need to have the signatures witnessed or notarized, though you can if you want an added degree of formality.

Writing down the details will require you to think through everything surrounding your agreement. In order to fill in the blanks, you will have to consider things that may not have come up before. Sure, your friends are welcome to stay at your lake house but did you discuss who will pay for the regular weekly cleaning? As you think about the specifics, you might realize that you really can't afford to do what you promised or that sticking to it will be difficult for you down the road. So often we find ourselves saying yes to people, only to realize that we wouldn't have agreed had we really thought about what was involved. The process of writing things down can help keep you from making a mistake.

Writing things down also helps you to avoid honest misunderstandings. When you have to write something down, you tend to be clearer about what you want. If the parties involved aren't thinking the same thing, writing out the details will help you recognize that and bring your expectations in line. For instance, when your brother says he will visit your elderly parents every weekend, does that mean he will spend all day Saturday and Sunday with them? And cook their meals on both days? When your daughter agrees to pay rent when she gets a "real" job, does waitressing count? Many times these types of questions go unaddressed when oral agreements are made because the parties weren't required to think through the details. Writing everything down compels you to address fine points and avoid unnecessary misunderstandings.

Memories fade. Five or ten years down the line it may be difficult to remember whether you agreed to pay 4 percent or 6 percent interest on the loan your uncle extended when you bought your first car. Or you may recall your mom saying you could leave your cat with her when you found your own apartment, but she may not remember saying anything like that. Me-ouch!

An agreement also helps when a misunderstanding isn't honest at all. It is harder to misrepresent history if that history is written down. You can't argue about whether something was a loan or a gift if you've got paperwork. Your best friend who goes off and sells your idea can't claim he didn't realize it belonged to you if you've signed an agreement. Your son knows that when he drives the family car he has to pay for his gas or lose the privilege.

Even if you have already made a verbal agreement with someone or are already part of an arrangement that you now realize could be fraught with misunderstandings, you can write down what has already transpired and what your expectations are for the future of the arrangement. For instance, your husband may have decided to move out, leaving the children in the family house with you, their mother. While this may have worked at the outset, when the kids were in school all day, now that summer is coming, the situation is more complicated. It isn't too late to draft a Shared Parenting for Separated/Divorced Parents Agreement and spell out how you want to handle school vacations, along with the other decisions that need to be made on the children's behalf. That way you can maintain a positive environment for the children with minimal daily conflict.

Filling in the Blanks

When you get down to the business of drafting your agreement, you will want to keep the following tips in mind.

TAKE CARE OF THE BASICS. First, make sure you use the correct names of the parties and that you date the agreement. You'll need to include everyone's current contact information. These details may sound simple, but they should not be overlooked.

BE THOROUGH. Next, you have to make sure you know what you want to say. Your agreement should answer all the critical questions: When? Where? How? How much? How often? Which ones? Under what circumstances? To whom? By whom? And, last but not least: What if? The agreements in the second part of the book should prompt you to ask the right questions. But there are probably unique circumstances that apply to you. Ask yourself questions even after you have filled in all the blanks, and add more details as they become necessary. You are not limited to what's in the form. Try to envision the situations that may arise and the types of problems that tend to make you the most agitated.

Once you are sure you know what you want your agreement to say, make sure you write it all down. An agreement should include everything you agreed on. Don't rely on your memory or believe that something goes without saying. Do not assume that the other person thinks the same way about something you didn't discuss. Just because your roommate has a car doesn't mean she will take care of all the grocery shopping for your shared apartment. You need to specify this upfront. Do not agree to something the other party mentions without putting it in the agreement. Say it all. Say it clearly. And don't take anything for granted. Then write it down!

BE SPECIFIC ABOUT TIME PERIODS AND DATES. When it comes to dates and times, the more specific you are, the better. For instance, in the case of a loan, it is best to specify an exact repayment date, like this: "The loan is due on or before May 1, 2020." While an exact date is better than simply putting in a time period, if for some reason you can't do that, you must be specific about the amount of time the borrower has to repay and when the clock starts running. It could be six months from the date of the signed agreement or six months from some other date or triggering event, such as from the time a person obtains a job.

If a loan is to be repaid in installments, you need to be specific about those as well. It is better to say "to be paid on the fifteenth of every month" than simply saying "monthly." You should also state when those monthly payments are to begin, how long those payments are to be made, and in what amount. An effective phrase is something like this: "to be repaid in the amount of $500 per month, on the fifteenth of every month, beginning on May 15, 2020 until the entire amount of the loan—$4,500.00—is paid off."

If you are loaning your vacation home for the holidays, you should specify that the loan begins on December 24 (of a particular year) and ends on January 2 (of the following year); otherwise "the holidays" could go on and on. Almost anything you do has some time component to it, so you have to consider that fact when creating an agreement.

TRIGGERING EVENTS. In general, the more specific you are about the time periods involved, the better off you will be. Sometimes, however, people agree on repayment of a loan after a certain event occurs, such as when the borrower receives his tax refund or when he gets a job. Triggering events can be a little risky. They require you to rely on outside forces over which you have little or no control. For instance, with respect to jobs and tax refund, you have to consider how hard a person is looking for a job or whether the tax refund money is actually due or is in the amount anticipated. Be as specific and clear as you can be when it comes to dates and deadlines.

AMOUNTS AND VALUES. You have to be sure that the agreement is clear on both amounts and values of items owed or exchanged. With a loan, stating the amount is usually an easy thing.

But what if you agree to take care of certain pet-related expenses? Is there a limit on how much you want to pay? If you agree to pay someone 10 percent of certain costs, are there going to be any upper or lower limits? If you lend someone a piece of your property and the borrower loses it, have the two of you agreed on its value? Lost property cannot be returned, but it can be compensated for. Remember that a lot of things have value, including work and time. So make sure you include the value of these things in your agreement, if that value isn't clear.

ACCURATELY IDENTIFY PROPERTY. If your agreement involves property of any kind, make sure that the agreement specifies exactly what that property is. For instance, if you loan someone something, include in your agreement a specific description of what it is. Let's say you are loaning your cousin Ann a dinette set. Don't just put the words "dinette set" or even "a chair and two tables" in the agreement. Either phrase could apply to any number of different dinette sets. You want to make sure you get back the very pieces of furniture that you loaned out, especially if they have sentimental value or are one of a kind. If it's the dinette set you inherited from Aunt Flo, you should say that. We suggest that you go even further. Remember that if the matter goes to court, the judge doesn't know anything about Aunt Flo or what her dinette set looks like.

Instead, you should describe the property in a way a third party unfamiliar with the property would understand. Consider language like this: "Aunt Flo's three-piece oak dinette set with red cushioned chairs and a square table." This gives a judge something with which to work. It's also advisable to take a picture and attach it to your document.

USE A SCHEDULE OR ATTACHMENT, WHEN NECESSARY. Of course, if the agreement involves a lot of property, you may not have enough space to list everything or fully describe each item in the agreement itself. That is when an attachment comes in handy. An attachment is a separate piece of paper, initialed by both parties, that can be used for additional information, including descriptions and photographic records. A schedule can be used to keep a record of dates and responsibilities, as you can see in chapter 13, the Roommate Agreement.

NOTE THE CONDITION OF THE PROPERTY. You should make sure that the parties agree on the condition of the property when it was loaned out or stored. That way there will be less room for argument regarding any damage that may have occurred while the property was in the possession of the other party. If your friend's car door is dented, make note of this before you borrow the car. Better yet, take a picture.

As we know, a picture is worth a thousand words. Placing in your agreement a picture of the item or the contents of a storage locker—together with a list of the locker's contents—is very helpful. It not only shows what's there, but also helps prove an item's condition. Again, any pictures should be dated and initialed by both parties.

DON'T JUST SAY *what*, **SAY** *how*. If there are several ways an action can be carried out, you need to specify exactly what you have in mind. This is often a bone of contention when people come to court. It becomes clear early on that the parties had two very different ideas from the beginning about how they expected a job to get done.

For instance, if your cousin is going to make some repairs to your home, you have to specifically state exactly what work is to be done. You can't simply say, "Fix the kitchen ceiling." That could mean a lot of things. "Patch the hole, prime, and paint," however, indicates the type and extent of the work. If you are asking someone to make something for you or do some work in your home, be specific. How long does the other person have to complete it? Do you get to approve the job's quality before the person gets paid? What about materials? Do you have the right to approve the cost of things before they are purchased and see all receipts for those materials?

In the case of a shared pet, ask yourself: Does training include housebreaking and obedience? Do you care if the cat's litter box isn't emptied daily?

If an adult child is moving back home, ask yourself: What will her household duties entail? What happens if he damages your property? Does keeping the house "clean" mean she has to mop the floors and scrub the toilets?

AGREE ON HOW YOU WILL KEEP TRACK OF THINGS. You also have to decide from the outset how you are going to monitor each person's compliance after the agreement is signed. Spelling it out in your agreement keeps confusion to a minimum and will provide you with evidence if all else fails and you end up in court. For instance, if you have entered into a loan agreement, a running account of repayment should be kept. If you and your siblings have agreed to take turns bringing your aging mother to the doctor, make sure someone is prepared to track her appointments and arrange for who is providing transportation each time. Use a schedule, along with your agreement, to log dates and responsibilities.

REMEMBER THAT YOU CAN EXCLUDE AS WELL AS INCLUDE. While many people take the time to consider everything they want to *include* in an agreement, oftentimes they do not realize that they have the ability to specifically *exclude* things as well. In other words, you can actually say what you *don't* want to happen or what actions will *not* satisfy the agreement. This can become very important if the parties interact a lot or if there is a whole category of property or things involved.

For example, if you are allowing someone to use your property or giving her access to items that belong to you, it is good to identify just how limited those rights are. You can say that a loaned car may not be driven out of town or over a certain number of miles (or km). Or that the use of a vacation home on a golf resort doesn't include greens fees and use of the golf cart. If you have a roommate and you just want to share space but none of your things, you can specifically say that the parties will not be sharing food and don't have the right to enter each other's rooms. You can say that neither party can have guests stay over for more than one night a week.

PREPARE FOR THE UNEXPECTED. Life happens. Things change. While your agreement cannot anticipate everything that might occur, it can address the most common contingencies. First, you must consider your own life and circumstances. What in your life is most likely to change that will affect the agreement? Your college graduate returning home will most likely *not* need to write anything into the agreement about having a child under your roof, while your married son and his wife living in your home might want to address that possibility. When you and your roommate get a dog together, you should anticipate that you won't be living together for the entire life of that dog. What will you do with him? Your friend agreed to pay back a loan month by month, but then loses her job. Your agreement should have a contingency clause covering that possibility.

Here are a few examples to consider:

- **WHEN TRIGGERING EVENTS DON'T HAPPEN.** As we discussed before, you can use a triggering event to signal when a loan will begin to be repaid. But what do you do if that event does not occur? (For instance, your daughter doesn't get a job or your brother doesn't get that tax refund.) You have to have a backup date. In other words, you should agree on a limited period of time in which that event must occur. Then, if the event does not occur, the loan becomes due on that date.

- **WHEN YOU BOTH WANT TO CHANGE THE AGREEMENT.** Sometimes both sides agree that an agreement needs to be changed. Part of the process of preparing for contingencies is deciding up front how you plan to revisit your document. Originally, you may have specified that your daughter couldn't drive at night, but now that she has a job at the mall, she will be working late. We recommend that you incorporate all changes to the agreement in writing.

- **IF ONE SIDE DOESN'T FOLLOW THROUGH.** Before you sign, you should also agree on the manner in which disputes will be resolved. Do you want to arbitrate or mediate the problem (we will discuss both ideas later)? Or rely on wise, trusted Great Aunt Gerty to listen to you both and help you work it out? Of course, you should make sure Aunt Gerty is willing to assume the role of mediator. Many family members wouldn't want to get in the middle of a family squabble. You should decide how formally or informally you want to handle things ahead of time.

- **IN CASE OF DEATH.** Grim as it is to think about, the agreements in this book provide a place to include a contingency in the case of this unhappy event.

Before You Sign

As a final check, you should give yourself time to take these steps before you sign the agreement.

READ IT OUT LOUD. Reading the agreement out loud will help you catch any mistakes or errors. Sometimes you write things down incorrectly. Sometimes what you wrote down doesn't make sense or is unclear. Other times you believe you addressed something because you spoke about it, but never wrote it down. Reading the agreement out loud will help you catch these mistakes.

ASK QUESTIONS. If you are not sure what everything on that piece of paper means, you should not sign it. If there is something you are thinking about, but it is not included in the written agreement, add it. Don't use words you don't understand and don't use terms that you heard on TV. The agreement should be simple and clear. If you do not understand everything in it or think it can be interpreted in different ways, ask about it and address those concerns in writing before you sign it.

ASK A THIRD PARTY TO READ IT. If you ask someone else to read the agreement before you sign it, he can catch things you missed. Or he may think of something that you have forgotten. A third party who looks over your agreement may identify a place where the two of you are making unexpressed assumptions.

SLEEP ON IT. Putting things in writing will also give you time to think them over. Before you sign an agreement, tell the other side you want to take it home and sign it later. That will give you the opportunity to decide if this is really something you want to do. It will also give you the ability to put the brakes on any high-pressure situations with pushy friends and or relatives.

After You Sign

You've signed the agreement, but be sure to do some basic follow-up to ensure that you're protected.

MAKE COPIES. Make sure both parties have a signed copy of the full agreement, including initialed copies of any addendums. The agreement should have numbered pages and state how many pages it contains, so everyone has all the information. Then you should make sure that you put the original agreement in a safe place and a copy of it somewhere else. After going through the process of writing it down, you wouldn't want to lose your documentation.

KEEP TRACK. If the agreement specifies that you must keep track of certain activities, that is exactly what you have to do and you must be consistent about it. If your agreement says you will keep a running account of repayment, you need to log each payment on a schedule. Entries that aren't included won't be considered unless both sides agree that they occurred.

While we want you to record as many details as you can and be as specific as possible, you also need to be realistic. Even with professionally drafted, multipage contracts, there is room for interpretation (or misinterpretation!). The courts are full of attorneys arguing about what various clauses mean. The message here is not to make yourselves too crazy trying to spell out each and every thing. We don't want the process to become so cumbersome or overwhelming that you abandon it. Remember, documentation of any kind is more than most people get, so you should consider it a victory that you took the time to write something down and put your name to your commitment.

CHAPTER 3

How to Enforce Your Agreement

Unfortunately, having an agreement doesn't mean that everything will go according to your written plan. Sometimes people simply don't comply. Other times, changes in circumstances make it difficult for them to do what they promised. Still other times, despite a written agreement, misunderstandings crop up.

This chapter explains how to keep an agreement in force. Renegotiation or a new attachment or an adjusted schedule may become necessary if there is a small problem or a change in circumstances. We also outline each party's options should the other party fail to live up to her promise altogether. Small Claims Court is the last place you want to end up, but should it come to that, you'll have your signed agreement to bolster your case.

Even with the best intentions and a well-written agreement, people may stray from the specific terms that seemed so clear when you started out. Your relationship may be strong and things may be going so well that you become comfortable relaxing the details. This is a mistake. Sticking to your agreement is vital. When sticking to it becomes too difficult for one or both parties, it is time to renegotiate some of the terms. What you don't want to do is let both parties drift from the original understanding without a discussion because then your agreement becomes almost impossible to uphold.

Perry's sister Jean needed a car for several weeks while hers was being repaired. Perry offered to loan her his Mustang convertible, since he could take the train to work. He said she could only use the car for work, and couldn't drive anyone else around. That was fine with Jean until her friend asked for a ride home from work one day. Jean called Perry to check and he said

okay. So Jean gave her friend a ride home every day that week. Although that isn't what Perry
had in mind, he didn't want to make a big deal of it so he didn't say anything. When her friend
wanted to stop for a drink on the way home, Jean thought that would be okay, too. But when
Perry saw his car at the bar, he was furious. Jean said that he did tell her she could drive her
friend home, so what was the big deal?

If one party is no longer abiding by your agreement as it was written, you need to do something about it.

The Easy Way

You may have a vision of you and your former favorite cousin standing in *The People's Court* duking it out, but you need to realize that running to court is neither your first nor your best option. In fact, there are a number of things that you should try before you go that route. Before you do anything, check your agreement. Read it over and remind yourself of the specifics. We all make mistakes—you may not be remembering things correctly. You also need to think about the issue from the other party's point of view. Is he technically in compliance? In other words, while he may not be doing things exactly the way you want him to, is he still doing what the agreement requires?

TRY SIMPLE COMMUNICATION FIRST. Once you have reviewed your agreement and decided that the other party isn't in compliance, try to work out the matter informally. Your first and best option is to communicate. Talk to the other person about your concerns. Maybe there is a simple solution to the problem. Maybe he has forgotten or misunderstood something.

Your initial conversation should be calm and rational. Ask questions before you accuse. Propose solutions instead of wagging your finger. So often in cases that end up in court, people are angrier about the other person's attitude than about the issue at hand. So talk to the person and do so pleasantly. You may be able to clear up confusion with a straightforward conversation.

If that is not the case, reread what your agreement says you would do if there is a problem. When you drafted the agreement you should have laid out a plan for this event.

WRITE A LETTER. If you are uncomfortable talking about the situation, or if you have tried talking and it didn't work, written communication is now in order. You might be tempted to fire off a quick, angry e-mail, but you are more likely to think through what you want to say and get better results with a formal letter. When you draft your letter you should have your agreement in mind. If this is your first contact with the person since the agreement was signed, your letter should be one of inquiry and gentle request in case there is a simple misunderstanding. You do not want to unnecessarily inflame the situation.

If you have already spoken and it is clear to you that the other person is reneging on what she promised to do, your letter should be firm. Refer to the agreement that you made and quote specifics, if necessary, to remind her of her obligation.

Remember, when writing a letter or an e-mail, it is always best to wait before you send it. Sleep on it so you are sure that the communication is designed to get results and not just blow off steam. You don't want to get personal or accusatory. By remaining businesslike and rational, you are more likely to get a positive response. Here are two sample letters to give you some ideas of the language you should and should not use.

An ineffective letter:

Dear Steve:

You are a complete *&^#*! How dare you hang up on me?! You owe me $1,600. I knew I shouldn't trust you. You better not have gambled it away again. I am sorry I even tried to help out a loser like you. Believe me, I am going to get my money one way or another. You better send it to me now or else.

> *Your ex-friend,*
> *Pete*

A more effective approach:

Dear Steve:

I am writing to remind you of the agreement we made on June 10, 2007 regarding the money you borrowed. In that agreement you said you would pay me $200 each month. I haven't received a check from you in eight months. When I called you to discuss this, we were disconnected. I don't know if you are having financial difficulties or if you have forgotten our agreement. Please call or write so we can talk about it. I would like to resolve this as quickly as possible.

> *Your friend,*
> *Pete*

Which letter would you respond to?

Formal Dispute Resolution

If an informal conversation doesn't work and you have sent a clear, direct letter but haven't heard back, you may need to pursue other dispute resolution clauses you put in your agreement. If you agreed that a certain third party would be consulted in the event of a dispute, you should bring that person into the matter now.

If you agreed to arbitration or mediation, then that is how you should go. You often see these terms used interchangeably, but they are different in their approach. You can find both arbitration and mediation services on the Internet and in your local phone book. Some arbitrators and mediators specialize in certain kinds of agreements, so you can look for those who have some experience in the matter at hand.

MEDIATION. Mediation is a process whereby an independent third party helps people who don't agree on something to resolve the dispute to their mutual satisfaction. Mediators will help foster a compromise. You can locate paid mediation services rather easily.

ARBITRATION. In arbitration, the people who are arguing present their problem to an independent third party and give that person the authority to make a decision. The arbitrator's decision, however, is only enforceable in a courtroom if the arbitration is *binding*. That means that the parties involved have signed an agreement that says they agree to follow or abide by the decision that third party makes.

ATTORNEY LETTER. If you cannot resolve things in an informal manner and, for whatever reason, mediation or arbitration is not an option or does not work, you might want to retain an attorney for the limited purpose of writing a demand letter. If you decide to go this route, you can expect that emotions will escalate and there may be consequences. Consider carefully how offended the other party may become to receive such a letter and how family and friends will view this action. You also need to make sure you know exactly what that attorney will charge you for the letter. You wouldn't want to spend $200 on a letter to collect a $50 loan.

Small Claims Court

Of course, if all else fails you can consider going to Small Claims Court. Small Claims Court was designed to give the public easy access to the court system. The average person can file a claim there without the aid of an attorney. However, it is not a cure-all. There are limitations and hidden costs to consider. You will be paying filing fees and will most likely lose time from work as you pursue your case. In most Small Claims Courts, the judge cannot award money for pain and suffering or other economic collateral damage, except in certain limited situations.

Even if you win in Small Claims Court, there is no guarantee that you will recover your money or property. All you get when you win is a judgment—a piece of paper that says, legally, Joe owes you *X* number of dollars. You still have to collect it. Sometimes people pay it right away; other times they do not. If they don't, you have to start a whole separate set of proceedings to garnish wages or access bank accounts. This can be another expense and headache.

If you feel sure this is the route you want to take, you will need to find out whether or not your local Small Claims Court can help you.

WHAT KIND OF CASES CAN I BRING THERE? The rules are different in every state. Generally, Small Claims Courts handle lawsuits in which one party is suing another for money under a certain amount. In some states, the most you can sue for is as little as $3,000; in other states, the limit is $15,000 or more. You have to check to see what the limits are in your state. If you are seeking more money than your local Small Claims Court allows, you have to bring your case to a court of general jurisdiction and should consult an attorney.

If the amount of money you are looking to collect is within the limits of what your Small Claims Court will award, the next step is to figure out if it is the *kind* of case your Small Claims Court will hear. Again, that varies from state to state so you have to do some research. Generally, Small Claims Courts won't hear eviction cases, libel and slander cases, or those involving the transfer of real estate. In addition, most won't give orders requiring a person to do specific things, like repair something. For the most part, judges in Small Claims Court just award money and, as we said, there is a limit on that. Many will not award money for punitive damages, like pain and suffering. There are exceptions, though, so you should find out what the policy is in your jurisdiction. For instance, some states have a Consumer Protection Act that includes a set punitive damage award for certain behaviors and Small Claims Court judges are allowed to make awards under that statute.

WHERE CAN I FIND ALL THIS STUFF OUT? The Internet is a good place to start. *Remember: You have to look for Small Claims Court rules within the state where you live.* Often, the state attorney general's office will have a guide to Small Claims Court that you can reference online.

Your local courthouse should also have those procedures, as will the state bar association. Remember, even in Small Claims Court, the plaintiff—the person filing the lawsuit—has to prove his case. Entire books have been written on this subject, and it is not our intention to go into specifics here. Just remember that when you go into court, you will need proof. In most of the cases brought to Small Claims Court, there is very little evidence to support a case one way or the other. The judge needs to rely on testimony from both parties. But if you took the time to put your agreement in writing, you have documentation to support your case and that could prove invaluable. During the course of your agreement, save all documentation, letters, ledgers, receipts, tapes—whatever might constitute a paper trail—so that you will have these backup materials if you need them.

Having written proof in the form of an agreement may be enough to keep you out of court entirely. And that is the real goal.

PART II

The Most Common Situations and Agreements

CHAPTER 4

Brother, Can You Spare a Dime?

The Lending Money Agreement

One of the most common (and troublesome) transactions between friends and family is borrowing and lending money. William Shakespeare warned us about it long ago. He said, "Neither a borrower nor a lender be." And while we all know how easily money can come between family and friends, sometimes you can't avoid it. If your sister's car breaks down and it is the only transportation she has for work, a small loan may be all that stands between her and unemployment. If you are a little short on your rent because of an unexpected expense, money lent from someone who can afford it may be the perfect solution. The trick is making sure the money doesn't come between the two people involved. A written agreement can help you avoid that kind of rift.

The first thing the Lending Money Agreement will do is help you decide whether making a loan is really a good idea. People usually lend money on the spur of the moment without thinking the whole arrangement through. There are a number of things both sides should consider. The lender needs to think about how much money he can really afford to give and how long it will be before he needs it back. Are there tax or estate consequences involved, depending on how much money is loaned or if one party dies while the loan is outstanding? Is the person you are about to loan the money to really in a position to pay it back and, if so, when? Do the two of you otherwise communicate well or do you have problems with that? The borrower should consider if she can pay the money back when she says and how she is going to manage to do that.

Barry loaned money to his nephew, Max, to buy a car. While Barry didn't need the money back right away, it was not a small amount. Unfortunately, Max wasn't the most responsible young *man. He decided that as long as Uncle Barry didn't say anything, he didn't really need to pay. Barry, on the other hand, didn't feel comfortable bringing the subject up. So whenever Barry and Max got together at family gatherings, there was always a $1,500 elephant in the room that no one wanted discuss.*

This entire situation could have been avoided if Uncle Barry had considered Max's reputation for slacking and his own lack of comfort in discussing money with family before he made the loan.

If you have considered the possible complications and decided that you want to make or get a loan, the second thing you must do is raise the issue of writing it down. Sometimes with family and friends we think that writing agreements down is unnecessary. After all, these people are close to us.

Unfortunately, often the opposite is true. We take liberties with those we love that we wouldn't take with others. If you don't pay Uncle John, there are no immediate consequences. If you don't pay your phone bill, your phone is shut off. Moreover, there is an increased level of discomfort when discussing money with family and friends. The phone company can hound you without worrying about insulting or upsetting you. But you have to see family and friends on a regular basis. It can make get-togethers uncomfortable for all.

Of course, if you are the one who needs to borrow money, asking for a written agreement is no problem. In fact, making the suggestion will probably help you get the loan. Offering to put things in writing will show that you are being responsible and intend to do the right thing. It will also help keep everyone on good terms until you can pay the money back.

Rob and Mary borrowed $6,000 from Rob's parents for the down payment on their first home. They were in the process of selling their van for that exact amount, so they only needed the loan until they could get the van sold. It was the longest four weeks of their lives. Rob's parents called every day asking about progress on the sale of the van. Rob and Mary were miserable the entire time and it was obvious that Rob's parents were miserable, too. If they had had a written agreement, it would have soothed Rob's parents and given Rob and Mary a specific period in which to pay the money back and avoid all the badgering.

Once you have decided that a loan is in order, you want to make sure that you are not only comfortable with the amount but that you have thought through all the ramifications of lending the money. If it is a small loan, say $200 or so, there might not be a whole lot to consider. But with larger loans, tax implications and calculating interest rates could become a problem. If you are lending a significant sum of money to someone, you should hire a lawyer and/or an accountant to walk you through the pitfalls. You might want to check to see how much money you can sue for in Small Claims Court in your state to help you decide if you should get outside help in putting together a loan agreement.

The Lending Money Agreement will ask each one of you what your reasons are for the loan. As a lender, you are entitled to know what the borrower wants to use your money for. While you might be more than willing to help your cousin with money for a car repair, you might not be interested in loaning the same amount so he can buy hot rod wheels and rims.

Everybody knew that Aunt Sue, a successful attorney, made a lot of money. As a result, Aunt Sue got a lot of loan requests. While she was happy to give her niece $1,500 to help her catch up on household bills when she was laid off, she was not at all willing to give her cousin Ralph the $2,000 he wanted. When she asked why he needed it, he hemmed and hawed until she got to the truth. He wanted the money as a deposit for a $14,000 motorcycle. She was not willing to make him a loan for that purpose.

Of course, no matter what people tell you, once they have the money you can't control what they do with it. Your real concern is getting paid back. In order to write things down, you have to decide and agree on a number of factors. When does the loan have to be paid back? Can the borrower pay it back in installments or in one lump sum? Will interest be charged and, if so, how much? How are you going to keep track of payments made? The Lending Money Agreement will help you address these and other details.

We understand, however, that some people may not want their agreement to have as many conditions as others, so you can decide which portions of the document you want to fill out and how many specific details you want to include. We recommend agreeing on as much as you can up front. For instance, it may seem that identifying the reasons for each person to get involved is not really necessary. But remember: Not only do you want to agree on the terms of a loan, you also want to preserve the parties' relationship as well. Filling out this section will help both the lender and the borrower understand their own and each others' motives so they can better address all relevant concerns.

The Failure to Repay section lets you specify what will happen if the loan doesn't get paid back as promised. Having an understanding with respect to what will occur under these circumstances will ease potential conflicts. If you have a procedure you both agreed on, the requests for payment made will seem less like badgering.

Of course, the agreement has no value if you do not fill out the Promise and you do not sign it. So at the very least, do that much. In the end, you should use the agreement to both the advantage of the borrower and the lender. Talk about and agree upon as many things as you can. The Lending Money Agreement is meant to establish harmony in a notoriously difficult situation. So with all due respect to Mr. Shakespeare, you *can* be a borrower or a lender, if you do it in the right way. The *right* way is to *write* it down.

FAMILY & FRIENDS AGREEMENT

Lending Money

PAPER HANDSHAKE · PRINTED PROMISE · PUBLISHED COMMITMENT

The Lender and the Borrower are making this Agreement because . . .

The Lender's reason(s):_____

_____

_____

(For example: To help you get out of debt; to help you further your education; to get you through a medical crisis; to help you start a new business)

The Borrower's reason(s):_____

_____

_____

(For example: To pay an unexpected vet bill; to continue my education; to help me buy a car; to get me through a monetary crisis; to help me handle a debt)

1. The Promise

I recognize that it is difficult to ask to borrow money and, after giving it thought, it is my intention to assist you in your monetary need. This document serves as an Agreement between both of us, the Lender and the Borrower, in order to make sure everyone is clear about the amount and terms of this Loan and to avoid any misunderstandings.

I, _____(the Lender's name), agree to lend you, the Borrower, the amount of $ _____.

I, _____(the Borrower's name), promise to pay back the total Loan amount of $_____, plus _____% interest (*0% if no interest is charged*).

I, _____(the Borrower's name), received the Loan in the amount of $ _____ on ___/___/20___.

The Loan will be repaid as follows:

❑   The entire Loan is to be repaid on or before ___/___/20___.

❑   The Loan will be repaid in installments. (Fill out section 4, "Installment Repayment Timeline.")

❑   And/or_____.

2. Contact Information

The Lender's name:_____
                         FIRST   M.I.   LAST   RELATIONSHIP TO BORROWER

Address: _____
            STREET   CITY   STATE   ZIP

Phone #: _____
            HOME   WORK   MOBILE

E-mail: _____

The Borrower's name: _____
                         FIRST   M.I.   LAST   RELATIONSHIP TO LENDER

Address: _____
            STREET   CITY   STATE   ZIP

Phone #: _____
            HOME   WORK   MOBILE

E-mail: _____

3. Manner of Repayment

The Borrower will repay the Loan in the following manner:

- ❏ Personal check
- ❏ Cashier's check
- ❏ Online bank check
- ❏ Electronic funds transfer
- ❏ Cash
- ❏ Other: Personal services or other items of value in exchange for cash, as described _____

  _____

- ❏ And/or _____

4. Installment Repayment Timeline

Loan to be repaid in installments until the loan is paid in full.

Installment Amount of $ _____ will be paid:

- ❏ Weekly—every Monday or _____.
- ❏ Monthly—the 1st or 15th of every month or _____.
- ❏ Annually on _____ (day/month)
- ❏ Per the following Loan Repayment Plan (both Borrower and Lender should maintain their own copies of whichever schedule is chosen)
  - ❏ Schedule A—Loan Repayment Plan and Record
  - ❏ Schedule B—Loan Repayment Plan in Place of Cash
  - ❏ Schedule C—Repayment for Loan with Interest
- ❏ And/or_____.

5. Communication

The Lender and the Borrower agree to notify each other in a timely manner:

- ❑ If the Borrower will be late or will miss a payment.
- ❑ If the Lender has not received a payment when due.
- ❑ And/or_____.

The Lender and the Borrower agree to:

- ❑ Keep the details of this Loan confidential.
- ❑ And/or_____.

6. If the Promise Is Broken . . . Failure to Repay

Grace Period and Late Fees:

A payment becomes late _____ day(s) after the due date. This is the Grace Period.

If the Borrower doesn't pay the amount due during the Grace Period, the Lender will:

- ❑ Charge a late fee of $_____.
- ❑ Charge a late fee of _____% on the overdue outstanding Loan.
- ❑ And/or_____.

Default:

If the Borrower doesn't pay the amount due within the Grace Period, the Lender may do any combination of the following:

- ❑ Allow the Borrower to work off the Loan in place of payment (See Schedule C, "In Place of Cash Payment").
- ❑ Give the Borrower a verbal reminder of the specific term(s) of payment.
- ❑ Send the Borrower a past due notice in the mail.
- ❑ Declare that the entire amount of the Loan is due and payable immediately.
- ❑ Never lend the Borrower money again.
- ❑ Seek mediation.
- ❑ And/or_____.

7. In the Event of the Death of the Lender or the Borrower

For these intentions to be formally and legally recognized, they must be entered into a valid will.

- ❑ In the Event of the Death of the Lender or the Borrower, see Attachment 1.

8. Signatures

A. We agree to take A Sane Approach to an Emotional Issue™. This Lending Money Agreement reflects our understanding with regard to our Loan. This Agreement replaces any previous agreements, oral or written, relating to the Loan.

Location where this Lending Money Agreement is signed: _____

CITY   STATE

The Lender: _____ ___/___/20___
                    SIGNATURE   PRINTED NAME   DATE

The Borrower: _____ ___/___/20___
                    SIGNATURE   PRINTED NAME   DATE

Witness (if wanted): _____ ___/___/20___
                    SIGNATURE   PRINTED NAME   DATE

INSTRUCTIONS:

1. Before signing, make a copy of the filled-in Agreement with any schedules or the attachment.

2. The Lender and the Borrower sign both the original, and the copy.

3. The Lender and the Borrower both keep a signed copy.

B. When the Loan is completely repaid, the Lender signs and dates below on both Lending Money Agreement documents—the Lender's document and the Borrower's document.

THANK YOU. THIS LENDING MONEY AGREEMENT IS NOW ENDED.

The Lender's signature _____ Date: ___/___/20___

Loan Repayment Plan and Record

Lender's name: _____

Phone number: _____

E-Mail address: _____

	PAYMENTS PROMISED		PAYMENTS COMPLETED			
PAYMENT #	$ AMOUNT DUE	DATE DUE (MONTH/DAY/YEAR)	$ AMOUNT PAID	DATE PAYMENT PAID	METHOD OF PAYMENT CASH*	CHECK NUMBER**
1						
2						
3						
4						
5						
6						
7						
8						
9						
10						
11						
12						
13						
14						
15						
16						
17						
18						
19						
20						

*All cash payments should be acknowledged with signature or initials of Lender.

** For check payments, keep record with check number.

Loan Repayment Plan—In Place of Cash Payment

Lender's name: _____

Phone number: _____

E-Mail address: _____

PAYMENT #	DESCRIPTION OF THE WORK	START DATE (MONTH/DAY/YEAR)	COMPLETED DATE (MONTH/DAY/YEAR)	TOTAL $ AMOUNT SERVICE OR ITEM REPRESENTS	ACKNOWLEDGMENT*
1					
2					
3					
4					
5					
6					
7					
8					
9					
10					
11					
12					
13					
14					
15					
16					
17					
18					
19					
20					

*All work should be acknowledged with the signature or initials of the Lender.

Repayment for Loan with Interest

Payment schedules and loan amounts with interest can be figured out by using a "loan amortization calculator." The calculator determines the monthly payment amount and all payment due dates. Each monthly payment amount includes principal and interest combined.

FIXED-RATE LOAN

Payment schedule for a fixed-rate loan with simple interest:

Borrowed amount	
Duration	
Number of payments	
Payment frequency	
Type of interest rate	
Annual interest rate	
Monthly payment	
Total interest loan	

LOAN PAYMENT SCHEDULE

PAYMENT #	DATE	PAYMENT AMOUNT	PRINCIPAL	INTEREST (PAYMENT AMOUNT MINUS PRINCIPAL)	BALANCE (BORROWED AMOUNT MINUS PRINCIPAL)
1					
2					
3					
4					
5					
6					
7					
8					
9					
10					
11					
12					

You can find an online loan amortization calculator on our Web site: http://www.asaneapproach.com/debt-calculator.

In the Event of the Death of the Lender or the Borrower

For these intentions to be formally and legally recognized, they must be entered into a valid will.

In the event of the Lender's death:

❑ The Loan is forgiven and the Borrower keeps the remaining money owed. It becomes a gift* from the Lender.

❑ The unpaid balance of this Loan will be deducted from any inheritance the Lender leaves the Borrower.

❑ The Borrower pays the remaining money owed to the designated Lender's Representative within ___ days of the Lender's passing.

❑ The Borrower continues to pay as stated in this Agreement to the designated Lender's Representative, until the Agreement is completed and the Loan is paid back in full.

❑ And/or_____.

In the event of the Borrower's death:

❑ The Borrower's Representative will use best efforts to pay back the Lender but will not be held liable.

❑ And/or_____.

Designated Lender's Representative's Contact Information

Name: _____
       FIRST   M.I.   LAST   TITLE

Address: _____
       STREET   CITY   STATE   ZIP

Phone #:_____
       HOME   WORK   MOBILE

E-mail: _____

Designated Borrower's Representative's Contact Information

Name: _____
       FIRST   M.I.   LAST   TITLE

Address: _____
       STREET   CITY   STATE   ZIP

Phone #:_____
       HOME   WORK   MOBILE

E-mail: _____

* Gift(s) may be taxed. Check with an accountant for further information.

INITIAL & DATE

The Lender's initials: _____ Date: ___/___/20___

The Borrower's initials: _____ Date: ___/___/20___

Witness' initials (if wanted): _____ Date: ___/___/20___

CHAPTER 5

It Isn't Mine to Keep?

The Lending Personal Property Agreement

You probably learned the importance of sharing before you could even recite the alphabet. It is a skill we're supposed to master by kindergarten. But when little Johnny broke all the crayons you lent him, there wasn't much you could do about it but cry. And not be his friend anymore. Even as adults, when someone breaks or loses something of ours, we may just want to cry. But with the Lending Personal Property Agreement in hand we can do better than that. We can share personal belongings with confidence because everybody knows what is being lent, by and to whom, in what condition, for how long, and what the consequences will be if something terrible happens.

For whatever reason, lending someone personal property sometimes seems easier than lending cold, hard cash. We do it casually all the time. *I've got a truck; you need to move furniture? Sure you can borrow it! I'm going to a black tie wedding; you've got the perfect pearl necklace? Great! I'd love to wear it.* However, it can also be a lot stickier. With cash, you know exactly how much you are giving. With objects, you don't really consider that the truck is your only form of transportation or that the necklace was your great grandmother's and is worth a lot of money (and has tremendous sentimental value). If something went wrong, there could be real trouble. Also, with loaned items, the condition always seems to come into question. Was that scratch on your coffee table when you gave it to your sister to store for you? Did the dress really look so *worn* when your cousin borrowed it? How do you account for normal wear and tear on an item when it is in someone else's possession?

When you borrow or lend personal property, writing an agreement leads you through these considerations and others in a way that doesn't become trivial or personal. Who wants to nitpick about whether a borrower took good *enough* care of something loaned? What an awkward conversation that can be for everyone involved!

For the sake of clear communication, this agreement, like all the others, has a spot for each of you to explain your goals. As the lender, your goal might be to help out a friend or to temporarily store something. As a borrower, your goal might be saving money or showing off a special family heirloom. Your goals may seem obvious, but you'll find that writing them down helps each of you remember "what is in it for you" and to move forward confidently.

The most important part of this agreement is the description of the item being lent/borrowed, or the "property." You should describe it as thoroughly as possible so that it is clear what the item is. Better than "a table and chairs" would be "an oak dining table with parquet inlay and six Windsor chairs with ivory upholstery on the seats." If possible, include the make, model, serial number, year, size, date of purchase, purchase price, original receipt, and whatever else helps identify the property. You should go into detail about the condition, too. If there is a scratch on one leg, write that down. If one of the chairs has already been mended, note that, too. You want to leave as little to question as possible when the borrower returns the item to the lender. We recommend that you take a photograph or a video to attach to your agreement to show the item and its condition.

> Sherri was going on an overnight camping trip with her daughter and the Girl Scouts but didn't want to invest in all the equipment just for the one night. Luckily, her neighbor, Steve, was an outdoorsman who was willing to lend her all the necessary gear. But Sherri wished she had taken a picture of the equipment before heading out into the woods with it. If she did, she could have shown Steve that his tent had a small tear when he gave it to her. Now she could only hope he had noticed it before he loaned it to her.

You will also specify the time frame for the loan. You'll remember our story in the Introduction about the loaned painting. A problem came up when Deborah and her husband wanted their painting back, but it had gotten very comfortable in its spot on her brother-in-law's wall. People get attached to things. Deborah's brother-in-law had found the perfect spot for the painting, but didn't realize that it wouldn't be hanging there forever. Everyone needs to know from the start that the loan is temporary. You will write down what the term is for the loan as specifically as you can. If you are letting someone use your truck for a weekend move, be sure to write down that you expect the truck back on Sunday night. Otherwise, you may not be able to get to work on Monday morning!

If there are conditions or limitations on how the property is used, spell those out in the agreement. The lender may not want his car driven out of state or he may allow no one but his brother to drive it—not his brother's girlfriend or anyone else. There is room to explain how, when, and where an object may be used.

Peter was selling his condo to take a job in another state around the same time that his buddy, Jeff, was moving into his first apartment. The situation was ideal. Peter wouldn't have to find long-term storage for his sectional sofa and king-size bed and Jeff didn't need to buy those big-ticket items right away. But Peter had allergies and wanted to be sure that Jeff wouldn't have pets in the apartment and on his furniture. He could specify that in their written agreement and there would be no question.

You will also need to discuss how the item should be cared for while it is in the borrower's possession. Of course, the borrower should be sensitive to the fact that this is the lender's personal property and it should be handled with care and consideration. But the lender should take the time to write down any special instructions or procedures he would like followed so that nothing happens to the item. Should it always be locked up? Is an alarm necessary?

Note that if the lender has serious concerns about the borrower's ability to protect her property, the lender can just say no, she would rather not loan something out. It is much less uncomfortable to say no now than to blame or resent someone later on. If something is irreplaceable and has such sentimental value that you can't imagine what you would do if something should happen to it, don't lend it. Even a written agreement won't repair the damage to a relationship if that is the case.

The bottom line with borrowing and lending is that there is some risk involved. Things get lost, broken, and stolen all the time. The Lending Personal Property Agreement helps you to spell out these possibilities and to decide on contingencies and consequences. Though we want to make our kindergarten teachers proud with our willingness to share, we also need to take care to protect our belongings and our relationships.

FAMILY & FRIENDS AGREEMENT

Lending Personal Property

PAPER HANDSHAKE · PRINTED PROMISE · PUBLISHED COMMITMENT

The Lender and the Borrower are making this Agreement because . . .

The Lender's reason(s):_____

_____

_____.

(For example: To share something that you need; to give you something to use until I need it back; to help you out with temporary transportation)

The Borrower's reason(s):_____

_____

_____.

(For example: To furnish my apartment; to hang something on my bare wall; to borrow jewelry to wear to a wedding)

1. The Promise

I, the Lender, agree to lend you, the Borrower, my Personal Property (described below). Because the Property has monetary and/or sentimental value, I ask for its safe return. This document serves as an Agreement between both of us in order to help avoid any miscommunications.

I, _____ (Lender's name), agree to lend you my Personal Property for your intended reason(s).

And I, _____(Borrower's name), agree to care for your Personal Property and to return it to you safely, per this Agreement.

Personal Property Description: _____

_____

_____

(For example: Great Grandmother's pearl necklace, in perfect condition; Maroon Chevy Blazer, 1998, dent in driver's door; 2000 Fender Acoustic guitar—newly restrung, one-inch scratch on face)

❑   To describe further, see Attachment 1, "Photographic Documentation Record."

The Lender will lend the Personal Property to the Borrower:

❑   on ___/___/20___ .

The Borrower will return the Personal Property to the Lender:

❑   on ___/___/20___ .

❑   Within ___ days of ❑ oral or ❑ written request from the Lender or the Borrower.

❑   And/or _____.

The Borrower will return the Property in the following condition:

- ❑ In the exact condition in which it was received.
- ❑ With regular wear and tear.
- ❑ And/or _____.

2. Contact Information

The Lender's name:_____
                               FIRST   M.I.   LAST   RELATIONSHIP

Address: _____
           STREET   CITY   STATE   ZIP

Phone #:_____
           HOME   WORK   MOBILE

E-mail: _____

The Borrower's name: _____
                         FIRST   M.I.   LAST   RELATIONSHIP

Address: _____
           STREET   CITY   STATE   ZIP

Phone #:_____
           HOME   WORK   MOBILE

E-mail: _____

3. Restrictions

The Borrower agrees on the following restrictions while in possession of the Personal Property:

- ❑ The Borrower will not lend this Personal Property to anyone else.
- ❑ The Borrower will keep the Personal Property safe at all times.
- ❑ The Borrower will never leave the Personal Property unattended in a vehicle.
- ❑ And/or _____.

Special Restrictions:

The Lender places these restrictions on the use of the Personal Property: _____

_____

_____.

(For example: Wear the necklace only to the prom and nowhere else; don't leave the guitar out in the sun, and keep only in its case; no other drivers allowed except for the named Borrower)

4. Personal Property Lost, Damaged, or Stolen

In the event that something happens to the borrowed Personal Property:

- ❑ The Borrower will immediately alert the Lender.

- ❑ The Borrower will immediately alert the police.
- ❑ And/or _____.

5. Failure to Return the Personal Property

If the Borrower fails to return the Personal Property in the agreed-upon manner:

- ❑ The Lender will give the Borrower a verbal reminder of the specific term(s) of this Agreement.
- ❑ The Lender will send the Borrower a notice in the mail and ask for the immediate return of the Personal Property.
- ❑ The Borrower will pay the Lender $ _____ if the Personal Property is lost, stolen, or otherwise remains unreturned _____ days after return date.
- ❑ The Lender will never lend Personal Property to the Borrower again.
- ❑ And/or _____.

6. In the Event of the Death of the Lender or the Borrower

For these intentions to be formally and legally recognized, they must be entered into a valid will.

- ❑ See Attachment 2, "In the Event of the Death of the Lender or the Borrower."

7. Signatures

A. We agree to take A Sane Approach to an Emotional Issue™. This Lending Personal Property Agreement reflects our understanding regarding loaned Personal Property. This Agreement replaces any previous agreements, oral or written, relating to the Personal Property.

Location where this Lending Personal Property Agreement is signed: _____
CITY   STATE

The Lender: _____ ___/___/20___
SIGNATURE   PRINTED NAME   DATE

The Borrower: _____ ___/___/20___
SIGNATURE   PRINTED NAME   DATE

Witness (if wanted): _____ ___/___/20___
SIGNATURE   PRINTED NAME   DATE

INSTRUCTIONS:

1. Before signing, make a copy of the filled-in Agreement with attachments.
2. The Lender and the Borrower sign both the original and the copy.
3. The Lender and the Borrower both keep a signed copy.

B. Upon the return of the Personal Property to the Lender from the Borrower: The Lender signs and dates below on both copies of the Lending Personal Property Agreement.

THANK YOU. THE LENDING PERSONAL PROPERTY AGREEMENT IS NOW ENDED.

The Lender's signature _____ Date: ___/___/20 ___

Photographic Documentation Record

PHOTOGRAPHIC AND/OR ADDITIONAL DESCRIPTIONS

Describe the Personal Property in further detail:

_____

_____

_____

_____

_____

Attach any additional documentation:

❑ Photograph(s) of the Personal Property (initial and date).

❑ Video of the Personal Property (initial and date).

❑ Further documentation (such as purchase receipts, registration, etc.): _____

_____

_____.

❑ And/or _____.

INITIAL & DATE

The Lender's initials: _____ Date: ___/___/20___

The Borrower's initials: _____ Date: ___/___/20___

Witness' initials (if wanted): _____ Date: ___/___/20___

In the Event of the Death of the Lender or the Borrower

For these intentions to be formally and legally recognized, they must be entered into a valid will.

In the event of the Lender's death:

❑ The Borrower keeps the Personal Property loaned. It becomes a gift* from the Lender.

❑ The Borrower returns the Personal Property to the designated Lender's Representative within ____ days of the Lender's passing.

❑ The Borrower continues along as stated in this Agreement, and returns the Personal Property to the designated Lender's Representative when the Agreement is fulfilled.

❑ And/or _____.

In the event of the Borrower's death:

❑ The designated Borrower's Representative will return the Personal Property to the Lender within ____ days of the Borrower's death.

❑ And/or _____.

Designated Lender's Representative's Contact Information

Name: _____
 FIRST   M.I.   LAST

Address: _____
 STREET   CITY   STATE   ZIP

Phone #:_____
 HOME   WORK   MOBILE

E-mail: _____

Designated Borrower's Representative's Contact Information

Name: _____
 FIRST   M.I.   LAST

Address: _____
 STREET   CITY   STATE   ZIP

Phone #:_____
 HOME   WORK   MOBILE

E-mail: _____

* Gift(s) may be taxed. Check with an accountant for further information

INITIAL & DATE

The Lender's initials: _____ Date: ___/___/20____

The Borrower's initials: _____ Date: ___/___/20____

Witness' initials (if wanted): _____ Date: ___/___/20____

CHAPTER 6

They're Back!

The Temporary Residence/Grown Child Returns Home Agreement

Grown children returning home is on the rise in America. In fact, it has become so commonplace, it now has its own name: "boomerang kids." And while there are probably a number of very good sociological, psychological, or economic realities that can explain this phenomenon, we are not concerned with that here. What this agreement is intended to do is to help take the tingle out of the boomerangs' return to the hands that sent them off into the world.

When adult children return home, it can be a difficult situation for all involved. For eighteen years, both parents and children have operated on the basis of one unquestioned belief: that parents are supposed to take care of their children, unconditionally and without hesitation, clothing, housing, and feeding them while expecting precious little in return. These roles are at the very heart of the way both parent and child look at the world and these deeply ingrained beliefs don't just vanish when grown children return home.

> *Samantha couldn't wait to finish college and go home. She was looking forward to a relaxing summer with her friends by the pool. Her parents assumed that she was going to spend the summer polishing her resume and going on job interviews. Little did they know that Samantha was tired of doing her own laundry and eating takeout, and was in no hurry to go anywhere. Six months later Samantha was still sacked out on the couch and her parents were wondering why they ever spent so much on college tuition.*

In order for this new relationship to work out, both sides must take the time to consciously shift their expectations. New ground rules set while completing this agreement will help both parties adjust to the fact that the child is now an adult—not just in terms of rights but responsibilities as well.

Moreover, many might contend that parents have a continuing obligation to their children to prepare them for the world. Or if you don't buy that, at the very least, they have an obligation not to get in their children's way. If parents allow a returning adult to readopt the lifestyle and responsibility level of a sixteen-year-old, they aren't doing her any favors. Mother birds push their chicks out of the nest for a reason. We have to do the same and see it as an act of kindness, not cruelty.

Likewise, if you are someone's child and trying to return home, an offer to put your intentions in writing might help you get back in the door. It will show your parents that you have matured and aren't looking to be taken care of again. It will also assure them that you are aware of their rights and space, and do not intend to disrupt their home.

Whether you are a parent welcoming home an adult child or you're an adult child returning to the nest, requesting a written agreement with someone so close can be hard. First we suggest that you make sure the other party understands what you are trying to do. If you are a parent, preface your request for an agreement with an acknowledgment of your love and respect. Tell your grown child upfront that you are doing this in order to avoid trouble. Let him know that boomerang situations have a history of going bad and you would like to keep that from happening. Even so, you need to approach returning children with a sense of businesslike resolve. For example, you can say something like this:

- I know things are tough; I love you and want to help.

- You can come back and stay with us, but I want to make sure this works out for everybody.

- I want you to feel respected as an adult but I also need you to respect my space.

- Let's put it in writing so everybody *knows what to expect.*

If you are an adult looking to return home, you might be more likely to get back in the door if you start the conversation with an eye toward calming your parents' fears. Make it clear you are not looking for a free ride and don't intend to stay forever. Say something like this:

- I'd like to come home but I want you to know that I am not looking for you to take care of me.

- I just need a little room until I get on my feet.

- I only intend to stay for a short period and I plan to contribute while I am here.

- I want to put in writing all the things I'm willing to do.

Becky moved out of her parents' home when she was twenty-two years old. She loved being grown up and on her own. Then when she started law school in her late twenties, she found it very difficult to work, pay her rent, and get her studying done. Her parents offered her her old room back, but at first Becky didn't want to accept. She didn't want to lose her independence. Eventually, she realized that it made sense to move home, but she insisted that she and her parents write an agreement that she would only stay until she graduated and that she would assume certain household responsibilities while she was there. Her parents thought that this was a mature approach and were happy to sign the agreement.

You should read through the agreement that follows, and its schedule, in their entirety before you start filling it out. That will give you an idea of the scope of what you need to talk about and may focus your attention on an idea peculiar to your household that you need to address.

It is probably best for both parties to put a limit on the length of the adult child's stay. It makes the parents feel less imposed upon and gives the adult child more motivation to get up and on his way. Or, you can put in a triggering event, such as when the adult child gets a job, saves up a certain sum of money, or finishes school. Remember, this can always be changed. You can discuss up front those factors that will allow the stay to be extended. If the grown child is demonstrating a sincere effort when it comes to lining up job interviews or obtaining good grades, or if she takes on additional responsibilities around the house, you may decide that another six months or a year would be fine.

You will want to establish whether or not rent should be paid. But before you discuss money with your child, you have to make sure you know how you feel about it yourself. Are you financially comfortable? Will having Junior around put a strain on your finances? Do you want to encourage independence? Does your child have the means to pay right now? Can the child contribute in other ways in lieu of rent? It is your right to decide how you would like to handle this. Remember, despite what your child may be telling you, you are not obligated to support him indefinitely!

The Kleins lived in a roomy four-bedroom house in the suburbs. They had plenty of space for their son and daughter to move home after college. But Mr. Klein had worked hard to achieve everything he had and didn't believe in making things too easy for his kids. So he insisted that they both pay a modest rent. They found this terribly unfair but agreed—they were still getting a great deal. What they didn't realize was that he was investing their rent money for them each month and that when they finally did move out, they would have a nice sum in savings to take with them.

Besides rent, you also have to discuss and agree on how you want to manage household and personal expenses. You may decide that it is unreasonable to ask the adult child to cover certain household expenses, such as utilities and groceries. However, personal expenses, such as grooming items and spending money, should be the child's responsibility. Don't forget to talk about insurance coverage. Will he need a separate policy for automobile, renters', and medical insurance? Or is he still eligible to be covered under the parents' plan and is there an added expense associated with that?

If you will allow your adult child the use of a family car, consider the following. Is there a limit on how many miles (or km) he can put on the car or what he can use it for? Can he leave the city or state with it? Must he ask permission to use it? Should he contribute to regular maintenance costs or just pick up the cost of repairing any damage he might cause? You don't have to allow the same access you did when he was in high school. It is your choice, and some restrictions might even encourage him to buy his own car.

As with household expenses, household duties can be a bit tricky. Regular chores can be seen in a number of different lights. They can be a contribution in lieu of money or serve to reduce the rent. Or they can be an expected adult responsibility. Even if the child is paying full rent, the parent and child need to discuss household duties. The parent is not running a hotel. When you are sharing common areas, issues of care will arise. You may insist that the grown child keep common bathrooms clean or his things out of the living room. The parent and child might take turns cooking dinner and cleaning up. You need to discuss these things up front and the agreement will help you do that.

Respecting that your child is now an adult, you should discuss your feelings toward guests and also how you view certain adult behaviors. Sometimes this is when the fireworks erupt.

Charlie had slept in his girlfriend Jen's dorm room every weekend since they started dating during their junior year of college. His parents knew about it, but never made any comment. So when Jen was coming to visit the summer after graduation, Charlie assumed that she would stay in his room with him. His mother would not allow it; she insisted that they sleep in separate rooms. Charlie didn't see what the big deal was.

Don't forget to discuss your thoughts about drinking, what you consider excessive partying, substance use, late night or overnight company, and any other behaviors that your child may be engaging in now that she has been out of your sphere of influence for a while. You can impose rules and guidelines as you see fit. You can even employ the old "not under my roof!" clause, if you would like. The point is to discuss these things ahead of time and be sure everyone is clear about the boundaries.

Oftentimes, little things become the largest bones of contention. Your home is your castle, and should be a place of comfort and contentment. So you have to make sure everyone knows what courtesies are expected in order to avoid undue irritations. While we have listed things you should consider, you have to remember that there are things that we cannot think of because they are *peculiar to you*. You need to take a moment and consider your personal quirks. Must the adult child keep his room clean or, if he doesn't, should he have to keep the door closed? Do you have this thing about people leaving dirty dishes in the sink? As the parent, do you want more privacy and insist that people knock before coming into your room? Does it bother you if someone else answers your phone?

It is important that you discuss the consequences for the failure to comply with the agreement. You may only need to review your document together and remind each other of what you had agreed on originally. Or you may realize that something needs to be revisited.

Recognize that your relationship will continue to grow and change, and some parts of your agreement will need to change as well. You may decide that when your daughter is earning enough money to pay for a closet full of shoes and two fancy vacations a year, she should start paying rent. Or you may see that your son is struggling to work part time and attend his business school classes, so you decide to pay his car expenses to help him out. At the heart of your agreement is the mutual respect and sincere intention to do right by the other person. If you both keep that in mind, every little detail of the agreement doesn't matter quite so much.

Temporary Residence/Grown Child Returns Home

PAPER HANDSHAKE · PRINTED PROMISE · PUBLISHED COMMITMENT

We, the Parent(s) and the Grown Child, are making this Agreement because . . .

The Parent(s)' reasons:_____

_____.

(For example: To help support you in a time of need; to provide living space during a job transition; to help in the transition from college to the working world)

The Grown Child's reasons: _____

_____.

(For example: To save money for my independent living; to get emotional support during a stressful time; to save money for a new home)

I. The Promise

I/we, your parent(s), am/are here to help you, and know that sometimes everyone needs a little extra time and support, but I/we recognize that both of our lifestyles may have changed. This document serves as an Agreement between us in order to avoid any difficulties or miscommunications that may arise as a result of this temporary living arrangement.

As the Parent(s), I/we, _____ *(Parent's name)*

and _____*(Parent's name)*, welcome you back to my/our home,

located at _____, and agree to treat you as an adult with respect and courtesy.

I, _____, the Grown Child *(Name)*, promise to respect my parent(s)' home.

The Temporary Residence begins: ___/___/20___.

The Temporary Residence ends:

❑   When it is financially feasible for the Grown Child to be out on his/her own.

❑   When the Parents or the Grown Child give _____ days' notice to conclude our Agreement.

❑   on ___/___/20___.

❑   And/or _____.

Rent will be paid:

❑   The Grown Child agrees to pay rent to the Parent(s) while living in the family home.

❑   The Parent(s) agree to allow the Grown Child to live rent-free in the family home.

❑   And/or _____.

2. Contact Information

The Parent(s)' name(s):

_____
FIRST   M.I.   LAST

_____
FIRST   M.I.   LAST

Address: _____
STREET   CITY   STATE   ZIP

Phone #:_____
HOME   WORK   MOBILE

E-mail: _____ E-mail: _____

The Grown Child's name:

_____
FIRST   M.I.   LAST

Phone #:_____
HOME   WORK   MOBILE

E-mail: _____

3. Finances and Shared Expenses

❑ The Parent(s) recognize that the Grown Child has an income and can contribute to rent and/or household expenses.

❑ The Parent(s) recognize that the Grown Child's income level may currently be low or nonexistent.

❑ The Parent(s) agree to provide him/her with $_____ per week/per month for a period of ____ months.

    ❑ This is a Loan to be paid back. (See The Lending Money Agreement.)

    ❑ This is a gift, an investment in your future.

    ❑ And/or _____.

Rent:

❑ The Grown Child will pay as rent the fixed sum of $_____, or _____ % of his/her salary on the _____day of each_____. *(For example, the 1st day of each week, the 15th day of each month)*

❑ Utilities are included in the rent payment ❑ Yes ❑ No

❑ If Utilities are not included in the rent payment, the Grown Child will pay the amount of $ _____ or _____% of each monthly Utility bill.

❑ If the Grown Child is unable to pay rent one month, after a discussion, we will do the following:

    ❑ Set up an alternative payment schedule for that month's rent.

    ❑ Agree to other responsibilities the Grown Child may take on in place of rent.

    ❑ And/or _____.

Transportation/Automobile:

- ❑ The Grown Child will pay his/her own automobile expenses, including car payments, insurance, gas, and maintenance.
- ❑ The Parent(s) agree to pay the Grown Child's automobile expenses, including:
  - ❑ Car payments.
  - ❑ Insurance.
  - ❑ Gas.
  - ❑ General maintenance.
- ❑ The Parent(s) agree to lend a family car to the Grown Child.
  - ❑ The Grown Child agrees to:
    - ❑ Consult Mom or Dad to schedule use of the car.
    - ❑ Never return the car empty, without gas. Gas tank should always be at least _____ filled.
- ❑ The Grown Child will pay the fixed sum of $_____, or _____ % of his/her salary, for use of a family car on the _____ day of each _____. *(For example, the 1st day of each week, the 15th day of each month.)*
- ❑ And/or _____.

Credit Card:

- ❑ The Grown Child will pay his/her own credit card expenses.
- ❑ The Parent(s) agree to cover all of the Grown Child's credit card expenses.
- ❑ The Parent(s) agree to cover all of the Grown Child's credit card expenses and the Grown Child will enter into a separate financial agreement between the Parent(s) and the Grown Child (see The Lending Money Agreement) to pay back the Parent(s).
- ❑ The Parent(s) agree to pay the minimum payment due monthly for _____ number of months on the Grown Child's credit card(s).
- ❑ And/or _____.

Health Insurance:

- ❑ The Grown Child will pay his/her own medical insurance and out-of-pocket medical expenses.
- ❑ The Grown Child will contribute the fixed sum of $_____, or _____ % of his/her salary toward medical insurance and out-of-pocket medical expenses.
- ❑ The Parent(s) agree to cover all medical insurance until the Grown Child's job covers him/her on ___/___/20___.
- ❑ The Parent(s) agree to pay the fixed sum of $_____, or _____ %, toward the Grown Child's medical insurance and/or out-of-pocket medical expenses.
- ❑ And/or _____.

Household Expenses:

Household Expenses include Food, Housecleaning, Telephone, Internet, and Cable.

- ❑ The Grown Child will pay his/her own Household Expenses.
- ❑ The Grown Child will contribute the fixed sum of $_____, or _____ % of his/her monthly salary for Household Expenses ❑ on the 1st of the month or ❑ _____.

- ❏ The Parent(s) agree to cover all Household Expenses or to cover all Household Expenses until ___/___/20___.
- ❏ The Parent(s) agree to pay the fixed sum of $_____, or _____ % of the Grown Child's monthly Household Expenses.
- ❏ And/or _____.

Move-out Expenses:

The Parent(s) agree to provide the Grown Child with:

- ❏ The gift of a security deposit for his/her apartment, up to the amount of $_____, when the Grown Child moves out.
- ❏ A Loan (see The Lending Money Agreement) to help pay move-out expenses.
- ❏ And/or _____.

4. Physical Contributions—Responsibilities

The Grown Child agrees to:

- ❏ Clean up after herself/himself and his/her guest(s) and pet(s) (if allowed).
- ❏ Do his/her own grocery shopping and food preparation.
- ❏ Do his/her own laundry and ironing.
- ❏ Contribute to additional household responsibilities (see Schedule A, "Household Responsibilities").
- ❏ And/or _____.

5. Space & Household Policies

Although we are all adults, we agree to some general policies for a clear understanding of our joint living arrangements within the household.

The Parent(s) agree:

- ❏ The Grown Child has a specific area to use as his/her space. That area is defined as _____ _____.
- ❏ The Grown Child may make alterations to that defined area, as specified below:_____ _____.
- ❏ The Grown Child may not make alterations to that defined area.
- ❏ And/or _____.

Pets:

- ❏ Pet(s) *(specify which pet[s])*_____ is/are allowed and the Grown Child is responsible for cleaning, feeding, caring for, and providing supervision for those pet(s).
- ❏ The Parents are not responsible for anything that happens to the Grown Child's pet while the Grown Child is residing in the Parent(s)' home.
- ❏ If the pet(s) become an issue, it/they have to go.
- ❏ No pets allowed.
- ❏ And/or _____.

Guest(s) and Overnight Guest(s):

The Grown Child:

- ❑ Is welcome to entertain up to _____ guests in the house at any given time.
- ❑ Will always check with the Parent(s) _____ day(s) in advance if he/she plans to entertain a large number of guests to make sure it works within the family schedule.
- ❑ Will check with the Parent(s)_____ day(s) in advance of having an overnight guest to make sure that it works within the family schedule.
- ❑ May not have overnight guests.
- ❑ And/or _____.

Overall Household Policies:

The Grown Child agrees:

- ❑ The garage belongs to the Parent(s). The Grown Child must ask for permission from the Parent(s) to use the garage before storing a car or any other of the Grown Child's belongings there.
- ❑ No smoking in the house.
- ❑ No drug use will be tolerated and it will be grounds to end this Agreement.
- ❑ Alcohol may be consumed in moderation if the Grown Child is of legal drinking age.
- ❑ For safety purposes, the Grown Child will keep the Parent(s) informed of his/her whereabouts.
- ❑ If he/she is coming home late or not coming home at all, the Grown Child will call and let the Parent(s) know, regardless of the hour.
- ❑ All preset family plans, including meals and other activities must be given _____ hours' notice if the Grown Child's schedule changes and he/she won't be present at home.
- ❑ And/or _____.

6. Additional Family Considerations

Due to the individuality of our family, the Parent(s) add the following considerations:

- ❑ _____.
- ❑ _____.
- ❑ _____.

The Grown Child adds the following considerations:

- ❑ _____.
- ❑ _____.
- ❑ _____.

7. Signatures

A. We agree to take A Sane Approach to an Emotional Issue™. This Temporary Residence/Grown Child Returns Home Agreement reflects our understanding with regard to the Shared Residence. This Agreement replaces any previous agreements, oral or written, relating to the Shared Residence. Upon signing, I/we welcome you back into our home.

Location where Temporary Residence/Grown Child Returns Home Agreement is signed:

_____
CITY   STATE

Parent: _____ ____/____/20____
        PRINTED NAME   SIGNATURE   DATE

Parent: _____ ____/____/20____
        PRINTED NAME   SIGNATURE   DATE

Grown Child: _____ ____/____/20____
              PRINTED NAME   SIGNATURE   DATE

INSTRUCTIONS:

1. Before signing, make a copy of the filled-in Agreement and schedule.
2. The Parent(s) and the Grown Child sign both the original and the copy.
3. The Parent(s) and the Grown Child both keep a signed copy.

B. When the Temporary Residence/Grown Child Returns Home Agreement has ended, the Parent(s) and the Grown Child sign and date below on both Agreement documents: the Parent(s)' document and the Grown Child's document.

THANK YOU. THE TEMPORARY RESIDENCE/GROWN CHILD RETURNS HOME AGREEMENT IS NOW ENDED.

The Parent(s)' signature(s) _____ Date: ____/____/20____

_____ Date: ____/____/20____

The Grown Child's signature_____ Date: ____/____/20____

TEMPORARY RESIDENCE/GROWN CHILD RETURNS HOME AGREEMENT, SCHEDULE A

HOUSEHOLD RESPONSIBILITIES

REGULAR CLEANING	FURTHER DETAILS	TIME LINES
	(For example: Washing laundry, including towels; cleaning kitchen, including emptying dishwasher)	*(For example: daily, weekly, etc.)*
Your room:		
Bathroom:		
Living room:		
Kitchen:		
Other		

ADDITIONAL WORK*

TASK DESCRIPTION	FURTHER TASK DETAILS	TIME LINES
	(For example: Rake all leaves, clean gutters)	*(For example: Daily, weekly, etc.)*

* Here you might want to consider yard work, home improvements, and errands as well as sharing educational or creative specialties in support of family goals and projects. You know your family best, so customize this form to encompass your commitments.

INITIAL & DATE

Parent's initials: _____ Date: ___/___/20____

Parent's initials: _____ Date: ___/___/20____

Grown Child's initials: _____ Date: ___/___/20____

CHAPTER 7

For the Sake of the Children

The Shared Parenting Agreement for Separated/Divorced Parents

When a couple separates or divorces, they can agree upon ground rules for care and custody of their children and present it to the court for approval. Or if they can't agree, the court can do it for them. Unfortunately the court does not love or know children as well as parents do. Nor can it provide detail on the everyday issues that come up when raising children. And while you are waiting for your case to go to court, you will have many occasions to interact on your children's behalf with the person from whom you are separating.

Parents who want to put their children first in this messy situation can use this Shared Parenting Agreement for Separated/Divorced Parents to establish a foundation for open and productive communication. Consistent and substantial contact by the children with both parents is a worthwhile goal, but it can be difficult to accomplish without getting into the emotional turmoil of the divorce or separation itself. For the sake of the children's emotional and physical health, both parents would do well to put their negative feelings aside and approach this agreement in a spirit of goodwill. It can be a powerful tool for effective co-parenting.

When Mike and Nancy split up, they both agreed that their first priority was making sure the children felt loved and secure. They promised each other that they wouldn't argue in front of the kids and that they would always try to remain friendly with each other. Very quickly they discovered that this was easier said than done, when every birthday, holiday, or special occasion put them at odds. They needed to work out a plan ahead of time, instead of relying on good intentions.

It may be difficult to be rational when the person who seems responsible for the havoc in your life challenges you. Anger and resentment may crop up every time your ex gives your child a gift or makes a decision on the child's behalf. This is understandable, but each negative exchange further undermines your attempts to provide your child with a stable environment. The more you can work out with your ex and write into your agreement, the fewer occasions for conflict there will be. You can determine in advance big things, like how you will approach education, medical issues, and personal safety, as well as seemingly smaller questions about hygiene, allowance, friends, and extracurricular activities.

Pat was looking forward to his weekend with his daughter, Megan. He planned to take her to his favorite restaurant for dinner and then to the movies. But when he showed up to get her at school, he almost didn't recognize her. Megan was dressed in a micro-mini with go-go boots and pink hair! There was no way he could take her out looking like that. What was her mother thinking, letting a 12-year-old go to school in that getup?

When you go through the many talking points in this agreement, keep in mind that you will need to make some compromises, too. This is an opportunity to voice your opinion and state your preferences, but it is your ex's as well. Things that you disagreed about when you were together won't be any easier to resolve now. But for everyone's sake including your own, you need to move on. Have the conversation. Hold your ground when something is vitally important, but be ready to give a little when you can. Always remind yourself that the agreement is about providing safety and stability for your children, not about your being right.

Maria didn't care that her ex-husband was seeing someone. She had gotten over it long ago. But she didn't think it was right for her children to have to cope with that on top of the separation. She felt that he should focus on spending time with his kids and not introducing them to his girlfriend. She hoped her ex would see her point, but she didn't want to risk an argument by bringing it up every time he picked up the kids. After some discussion, they were able to agree that for the first six months of the separation he wouldn't see his girlfriend during his evenings and weekends with the kids.

In your agreement you should also spell out the ground rules for ongoing communication. You may quickly see that a conversation on the doorstep when passing the children between you is not the most comfortable or effective way to talk. You will have issues that come up with your children. You can decide whether you would prefer to meet for coffee once a month or to talk by telephone regularly. Maybe your relationship has disintegrated to the point that e-mail is the only way you can exchange information without emotions erupting.

You may need to stipulate that your ex is never to call you at work unless the call involves a life or death emergency. It is essential for both of you to be available and open to communication in some way, and to let each other know what form that communication will take.

When a marriage breaks up, there is a strong emotional undercurrent and even a great agreement won't make all the anger, hurt, and disappointment disappear. Those are emotions that you and your ex will each have to deal with over time. We applaud you for taking this huge step to minimize day-to-day conflict with each other and set up the best situation for raising your children together by working through the process of writing a Shared Parenting Agreement.

Of course, any court order relating to issues of support and visitation involving the children must be followed. While you can request a modification of the order, you cannot change it unilaterally. Still, courts welcome parents who have resolved issues on their own, especially with respect to the children. If you and you ex are able to put together a reasonable agreement and present it to the court, the court will probably issue an order based on it. If you and your ex are unable to sit down rationally and put a Shared Parenting Agreement together, there are divorce mediators who can help you get past resentments and on to resolutions that work for everyone involved.

Shared Parenting for Separated/Divorced Parents

PAPER HANDSHAKE • PRINTED PROMISE • PUBLISHED COMMITMENT

As Parents, we are making this Agreement because:

Mom: _____

_____

Dad: _____

_____

(For example: To ensure that our child is taken care of in the best possible way, given the situation; to maintain a healthy relationship with the mother/father of my child in any way that I can)

I. The Promise

When it comes to our Children, let's put aside any of our personal differences, and solely work toward his/her/their well-being. This document serves as an Agreement about shared parenting between Parents, Mom and Dad.

Parents may have one child, or multiple children to include in this Shared Parenting Agreement for Separated/Divorced Parents. This document refers only to the plural, *Children,* to keep it easy to read. If you have one child, please fill in the Children sections for your one child.

As Parents, we, _____ *(Mom's name)* and _____ *(Dad's name),* agree to treat one another with respect and common courtesy and seek winning solutions for our Children. We also agree to provide a stable, consistent, loving, safe, and emotionally secure environment for our Children.

The Children's name and dates of birth: _____

_____

_____

_____

The Shared Parenting Agreement begins: ___/___/20___.

The Shared Parenting Agreement ends:

❑ on ___/___/20___.

❑ When the Children reach their 18th birthdays.

❑ When the Children graduate from high school.

❑ And/or _____.

Parenting Plan:

❑ Parents agree to pursue joint legal custody.

❑ Parents agree that ❑ Mom or ❑ Dad will be the only Residential Parent (the Parent the Children live with, except for visitation).

❏ Parents agree that Mom and Dad are Co-Residential Parents (the Children will live with each parent an equal amount of time).

❏ And/or _____ .

2. Contact Information

Mom's name: _____
              FIRST   M.I.   LAST

Address: _____
         STREET   CITY   STATE   ZIP

Phone #:_____
         HOME   WORK   MOBILE

E-mail: _____

Dad's name: _____
              FIRST   M.I.   LAST

Address: _____
         STREET   CITY   STATE   ZIP

Phone #:_____
         HOME   WORK   MOBILE

E-mail: _____

❏ For Emergency Contact List, see Attachment 1.

3. Contact and Visitation

Parents agree that the Nonresidential Parent will:

❏ Have the right to contact the Children by telephone _____ *(number)* of times per week.

❏ Have visitation every other weekend.

❏ See Schedule A, "Contact and Visitation—Detailed Choices," to specify contact and visitation in more detail.

Parents agree that each Parent will:

❏ Provide complete current contact information for each other as well as for the Children's health care professionals, schools, and babysitters. Parents also agree to promptly inform each other of any change in contact information.

❏ Inform the other Parent if the Children spend more than ___ nights away from home in a ❏ week or ❏ month, when that is, and the address and phone # where the Children can be reached while they are staying overnight.

❏ Immediately inform the other Parent of the Children's urgent issues, medical needs, and emergencies.

❏ Update the other Parent promptly about the Children's school activities, including all progress reports, report cards, events, sports participation, teacher meetings/conferences, and problems.

❏ Regularly call to discuss how the Children are doing at these times: _____ .
(For example: every Wednesday; twice a month, on the 1st and the 15th, at 7:30 p.m.)

❏ And/or _____ .

4. Holidays & Vacations

- ❑ Parents will alternate holidays.
- ❑ Parents will split holidays.
- ❑ And/or _____.
- ❑ See Schedule B, "Vacation and Holiday Schedule—Detailed Choices," to specify holiday and vacation choices in more detail.

5. Decision Making

Parents will make decisions with the best interests of the Children in mind. Parents agree:

- ❑ That day-to-day parenting decisions will be made by the Parent the Children are living with at the time.
- ❑ OR to follow Schedule C, "Decision Making: Our Children's Day-to-Day Rules and Routines," which specifies, in detail, day-to-day parenting decisions like treatment of minor health problems and injuries, diet, and discipline.
- ❑ That all major parenting decisions will be made jointly.
- ❑ That major parenting decisions will be made by the Parent the Children are living with at the time. (See Schedule D, "Decision Making: Major Parenting Decisions," to specify, in detail, major parenting decisions, like major medical, dental, or psychological decisions.)
- ❑ And/or _____.

6. Finances and Shared Expenses

Child support

- ❑ Parents agree that ❑ Mom or ❑ Dad will give to ❑ Mom or ❑ Dad $_____ per ❑ week or ❑ month toward support of the Children:
  - ❑ until _____ (date).
  - ❑ until court-ordered support is decided.
  - ❑ until otherwise agreed (_____).
- ❑ Parents will abide by the court-approved Child Support Agreement or Child Support Order.

Parents will discuss a mutually agreeable approach to spending money for the Children's well-being.

- ❑ Parents agree that the Parent with whom the Children are living at the time will pay for necessities. *(For example, food, housing, medicine, transportation, toiletries)*
- ❑ And/or _____.

Parents will consult each other regarding major expenses, which are expenditures over $ ___ per item or over $ ___ ❑ per week or ❑ per month. Parents will agree on major expenses before the money is spent.

(Major expenses can be defined as major medical and major dental procedures, such as braces and retainers, private school costs, camps, extracurricular costs, or anything over the decided amount above.)

- ❑ And/or _____.

7. Acknowledgments

Parents acknowledge:

- ❑ Our Children's need to spend time with the Other Parent.
- ❑ Our Children's need to love the Other Parent.
- ❑ The need for both Parents to stay connected with our Children.

- ❏ That our Children's well-being is our most important goal when it comes to shared parental decisions.
- ❏ And/or _____.

Parents acknowledge that our Children are Children and agree:

- ❏ To ensure that our Children aren't caught in the middle of adult situations.
- ❏ To seek emotional support from other adults, not from our Children.
- ❏ To discuss disputed issues with the other Parent out of sound and sight range of our Children.
- ❏ To shelter our Children from harm, from witnessing inappropriate behavior, from verbal or physical threat.
- ❏ To encourage our Children to engage with age-appropriate friends and participate in positive activities and continue with their usual interests.
- ❏ To do what they say we'll do, honor agreements, including schedules.
- ❏ To speak positively about the Other Parent and his/her family and friends, or make no comment at all.
- ❏ To support our Children's loyalties to other Parent and the Other Parent's family members.
- ❏ And/or _____.

8. Signatures

A. We agree to take A Sane Approach to an Emotional Issue™. This Shared Parenting Agreement reflects our understanding with regard to parenting our Children.

We will abide by this Agreement unless, or until, there is a court order issued regarding shared custody.

Location where Shared Parenting Agreement is signed:

_____
CITY   STATE

Mom: _____ ___/___/20___
            PRINTED NAME   SIGNATURE   DATE

Dad: _____ ___/___/20___
            PRINTED NAME   SIGNATURE   DATE

Witness: _____ ___/___/20___
            PRINTED NAME   SIGNATURE   DATE

INSTRUCTIONS:

1. Before signing, make a copy of the filled-in Agreement with any schedules and attachments.
2. Mom and Dad both sign both the original and the copy.
3. Mom and Dad both keep a signed copy.

B. When the Shared Parenting Agreement has ended, Parents sign and date below on both documents: Dad's document and Mom's document.

THANK YOU. THE SHARED PARENTING AGREEMENT IS NOW ENDED.

Mom's signature:_____ Date: ___/___/20 ___

Dad's signature:_____ Date: ___/___/20 ___

Contact and Visitation—Detailed Choices

Decide the details of the visitation and contact schedule for you and your Children. Examples are given in italics.

VISITATION SCHEDULE

MOM	DAD	VISITATION	FURTHER VISITATION DETAILS (For example: When/where this will take place; how long; which days of the week)
	X	*Every other weekend* (start date ___/___/20___)	*(For example: Dad will pick up Children from school on Friday and return to Mom by Sunday at 5:00 p.m.)*
	X	*Every Wednesday* (start date ___/___/20___)	*(For example: Dad will pick up Children after school for dinner and have them home by 7:30 p.m.)*

CONTACT SCHEDULE

MOM	DAD	CONTACT (Fill out in addition to visitation)	FURTHER CONTACT DETAILS (Fill out in addition to visitation)
X		*Will call our Children every day.*	*(For example: Call will be made between 7:30 p.m. and 8:30 p.m.)*

INITIAL & DATE

Mom's initials: _____ Date: ___/___/20___ Dad's initials: _____ Date: ___/___/20___

Vacation and Holiday Schedule: Detailed Choices

Please fill out the details of the annual holiday and vacation schedule for you and your Children.

MOM	DAD	VACATION/HOLIDAY	FURTHER DETAILS *(For example: Who will pick up and drop off the Children, at what location; for how long; split equally or use percentages)*
		New Year's Day	
		Dr. Martin Luther King, Jr. birthday	
		President's Day weekend	
		Spring break	
		Mother's Day	
		Memorial Day weekend	
		Father's Day	
		Summer break	
		July 4th	
		Labor Day weekend	
		Columbus Day	
		Halloween	
		Veteran's Day weekend	
		Fall break	
		Thanksgiving Day	
		Winter break	
		Child's birthday	
		Mother's & Father's birthdays	
		Other:	
		Other:	

INITIAL & DATE

Mom's initials: _____ Date: ___/___/20____ Dad's initials: _____ Date: ___/___/20____

Decision Making: Our Children's Day-to-Day Rules and Routines

Please fill in details of your Children's day-to-day rules and routines.*. Examples are given in italics below.

MOM AND DAD BOTH AGREE	DAY-TO-DAY RULES AND ROUTINES	FURTHER DETAILS
	Diet	
	Our Children can have ____ treat(s) per day	*(1 chocolate bar)*
	Health Problems	
	Behavior/Discipline	
	Routines	

*Consider food choices, rest and play preferences, homework expectations as well as use of equipment/technology and expectations surrounding conflict resolution.

INITIAL & DATE

Mom's initials: _____ Date: ___/___/20____   Dad's initials: _____ Date: ___/___/20____

Decision Making: Major Parenting Decisions

Please fill out details regarding how you will deal with major parenting decisions. Examples in italics below.

MOM AND DAD BOTH AGREE	MAJOR CONCERNS	FURTHER DETAILS
	Medical	
	We will contact the Other Parent to make medical decisions together.	*If he/she is unavailable, the available parent has the right to make a choice.*
	Dental	
	Emotional	
	Other	

INITIAL & DATE

Mom's initials: _____ Date: ____/____/20____   Dad's initials: _____ Date: ____/____/20____

Emergency Contact List

EMERGENCY CONTACT PHONE NUMBERS

Mom

Contact: _____ Relationship to Mom: _____

Phone #: Home:_____ Work: _____ Mobile: _____

Dad

Contact: _____ Relationship to Dad: _____

Phone #: Home:_____ Work: _____ Mobile: _____

CONTACT INFORMATION FOR CHILDREN'S DOCTORS

Child's Name: _____

Contact:_____ Specialty:_____

Office address: _____ Phone #: _____

Contact:_____ Specialty:_____

Office address: _____ Phone #: _____

Child's Name: _____

Contact:_____ Specialty:_____

Office address: _____ Phone #: _____

Contact:_____ Specialty:_____

Office address: _____ Phone #: _____

Child's Name: _____

Contact:_____ Specialty:_____

Office address: _____ Phone #: _____

Contact:_____ Specialty:_____

Office address: _____ Phone #: _____

CHAPTER 8

Siblings Unite!

The Caring for Our Aging Parents Agreement

Adult children are often called on to care for their aging parents. They may need to do as little as handling grocery shopping and driving the parent to the doctor occasionally. Or they may need to have their parent move in with them and provide full-time care. Either way, the situation may be difficult, and when siblings are involved, things can become confusing and contentious. Old family dynamics and emotional issues can kick in during times of crisis. However, if you take time to sit down and fill out this agreement, you can turn this difficult time into an opportunity to strengthen family bonds.

> *Eileen, who had never married, lived with her mother since graduating from college twenty-five years earlier. It was a nice arrangement, providing Eileen with the comfort of the family home and providing her mother with companionship after the death of Eileen's father. But as her mother got older, Eileen found her responsibilities growing. She had a full-time job and it was becoming increasingly difficult to handle her mother's care on her own. Luckily, Eileen was one of seven children, so there were other people who could help. The challenge was telling her brothers and sisters what she needed.*

First and foremost, this agreement will provide you with a blueprint for a conversation among siblings about the best way to take care of your mother and/or father as they age. It will prompt discussion on issues none of you may have considered yet, as well as help you figure out how to handle those things that you may be anticipating. Perhaps your mother is still well and living on her own, but the family would all feel more comfortable with a plan for regular, consistent contact. Or your father has gotten into a car accident and it is clear that he shouldn't be driving anymore, even though he is otherwise healthy and independent. And which sibling is prepared, should it become necessary, to provide financially for your parents?

The reality of parents growing older can creep up on adult children, especially if no specific illness is involved. One day your parents may be traveling the world, and then suddenly it seems as if getting around town poses a challenge. A child who lives nearby may begin to drive them around occasionally but as the parents age, and their need for transportation increases, that child may become overwhelmed. By preparing for this eventuality, adult children can avoid finding themselves in an arrangement that is too big a burden or is inherently unfair. While your brother on the opposite coast can't be expected to drive your parents to their doctors' appointments, once he recognizes the need, he can help provide a solution. Perhaps he can help pay for a car service or he might schedule more frequent and longer visits to give you a break. Sometimes the simple acknowledgment of how much responsibility one sibling has taken on over the months and years can take the sting out of the situation.

> Rose lived in her own apartment down the street from her son, Jeff, and his wife, Rachel. Jeff and Rachel had dinner with Rose at least twice a week and Rachel often stopped by in between to say "hello" and drop off milk or dry cleaning. When Rose had the flu, Rachel began to do Rose's laundry and some housekeeping. Then after Rose fell and broke her hip, Rachel would check in on her daily. She loved Rose and was happy to do it, but she couldn't help feeling some resentment that Rose's own daughter, Sharon, hardly came at all. And Sharon never even thanked Rachel for all she was doing.

Working through the agreement when one or both parents are still relatively well and independent should help each family member realize what will be involved down the road. At this point it may be wise to designate someone to accompany Mom or Dad on doctors' appointments to be sure the family is clear on the parents' health status. Another sibling might take on the task of working with parents on their financial plan and legal affairs. Communication at this stage can save a lot of grief later on.

When a parent becomes ill or incapacitated, the need for siblings to come together on behalf of the parent is more immediate and acute. The Caring for Our Aging Parents Agreement is flexible, so that you'll be able to designate a primary caregiver, if necessary, or assign duties to different siblings. If a parent needs to move in with a sibling, the agreement helps to spell out what responsibilities are to fall entirely on that sibling and how the other siblings will contribute. A very important section arranges rest periods for the primary caregiver. Whether other siblings come and live with the parent or have the parent come live with them for a specified period, it is clear up front that the primary caregiver is not alone and the role she has assumed is not taken for granted by the other siblings.

The next section of the agreement helps sort out the potentially messy issue of money. Even parents who are financially secure when they retire at sixty-eight may need assistance by the time they reach ninety. And health care expenses, on top of regular living expenses, can become very costly. It can help ease everyone's mind to have the discussion, learn what Mom and Dad have set aside, and get a sense of what everyone is prepared to contribute financially toward keeping their parents comfortable.

Marla's mom did a great job of juggling her finances, but she simply could not keep up with her medical expenses, rent, clothes, and groceries on her fixed income. Marla's dad had died years earlier and her mom had been using her savings to make ends meet. Her savings were almost depleted and she had many years of life left. She had just taken a fall, been diagnosed with dementia, and could no longer live by herself. Her children were all over the country and though they were all willing to help in their own way, old family dynamics kicked in. The squabbling began as to who would take over managing Mom's limited finances and who would contribute what to her continuing care. Could they all afford to put her in an assisted-living facility? Did Marla want her mom to move in with her so she could care for her herself? Decisions needed to be made immediately.

This agreement will also guide siblings in establishing how major decisions will be made regarding their parents, should the parents be unable to make such decisions for themselves. Sometimes these decisions need to be made quickly, and having a system in place facilitates this.

Of course, all siblings will want to be kept in the loop on the well-being and ongoing care of their parent(s). In this agreement they can specify how they would like this to be done. Working on the agreement together is a way to open lines of communication. Signing it is a testament to each sibling's commitment to their parents and to each other that they will work together, talk things out, and keep their family united.

Caring for Our Aging Parents

PAPER HANDSHAKE · PRINTED PROMISE · PUBLISHED COMMITMENT

As siblings, we are making this Agreement because . . .

Sibling 1: _____

_____

_____

Sibling 2: _____

_____

_____

Sibling 3: _____

_____

_____

Sibling 4: _____

_____

_____

(For example: To ensure that Our Mother/Father is/are being taken care of in the best possible way as they age; to maintain a harmonious relationship with my siblings during this time; to share caregiver responsibilities fairly; to create a plan before Our Parents need help)

I. The Promise

Let's be prepared to help Our Parent(s) as they age, by working together toward his/her/their well-being, and supporting one another in that effort. This document serves as an Agreement between Siblings, about the caregiving of Our Parent(s).

As Siblings, we, _____ (Sibling 1's name), _____

(Sibling 2's name), _____ *(Sibling 3's name), and* _____

(Sibling 4's name) agree to share the responsibility for caring for Our Parent(s)_____

(Parent's name) and _____ *(Parent's name)* as he/she/they age and support them in

their wishes as much as we are able. We also agree to respect and support one another in this time of

Our Parent(s)' needs.

❑ If there are more than four siblings, fill out Attachment 1.

The Caring for Our Aging Parents Agreement begins: ___/___/20___

The Caring for Our Aging Parents Agreement ends: ___/___/20___

❑ And/or _____.

2. Contact Information

Sibling 1: _____
FIRST   M.I.   LAST   RELATIONSHIP

Address: _____
STREET   CITY   STATE   ZIP

Phone #: _____
HOME   WORK   MOBILE

E-mail: _____

Sibling 2: _____
FIRST   M.I.   LAST   RELATIONSHIP

Address: _____
STREET   CITY   STATE   ZIP

Phone #: _____
HOME   WORK   MOBILE

E-mail: _____

Sibling 3: _____
FIRST   M.I.   LAST   RELATIONSHIP

Address: _____
STREET   CITY   STATE   ZIP

Phone #: _____
HOME   WORK   MOBILE

E-mail: _____

Sibling 4: _____
FIRST   M.I.   LAST   RELATIONSHIP

Address: _____
STREET   CITY   STATE   ZIP

Phone #: _____
HOME   WORK   MOBILE

E-mail: _____

For additional Sibling contact information, see Attachment 1.

3. For Parent(s) Living on Their Own

Day-to-Day Living:

❑ Siblings agree that Our Parent(s) need the following day-to-day care:

   ❑ Daily visits to ensure health and welfare.

- ❑ Daily telephone contact to ensure health and welfare.
- ❑ Assistance with medical care/doctors visits.
- ❑ Assistance with medication.
- ❑ Assistance with transportation, shopping, etc.
- ❑ Assistance with legal affairs including Living Wills and Will.
- ❑ And/or:
- ❑ Sibling # _____ (the Primary Caregiver) will be primarily responsible for overseeing the day-to-day care of Our Parent(s).
- ❑ Sibling #s _____, as Secondary Caregivers, will share responsibility for Our Parent(s)' day-to-day care as provided on Schedule A, "Sharing Responsibilities."

4. For Parent(s) Living with a Sibling

Day-to-Day Living:

- ❑ Sibling # _____ is the Primary Caregiver and Our Parent(s) will live at the Primary Caregiver's residence.
- ❑ Sibling # _____ is the Primary Caregiver and will live with Our Parent(s) at the parental home.
- ❑ Parent(s) will live with each sibling as follows:

  Sibling 1: _____

  Sibling 2: _____

  Sibling 3: _____

  Sibling 4: _____

- ❑ The Primary Caregiver will be responsible for the day-to-day needs when Parent(s) is/are living with them.
- ❑ The Primary Caregiver has the power to make day-to-day decisions regarding the welfare of Our Parents.
- ❑ The Primary Caregiver shall be assisted by the Other Siblings as indicated on Schedule A, "Sharing Responsibilities."
- ❑ And/or _____

Rest for the Primary Caregiver:

- ❑ Siblings agree to give the Primary Caregiver _____ # of rests per year..
- ❑ See Schedule B, "Rest for the Primary Caregiver and Visiting," to specify choices in more detail.

5. Finances

Routine Expenses

- ❑ Sibling 1 will give to the Primary Caregiver $ _____ per ❑week or ❑month toward Our Parent(s)' Routine Expenses:*
- ❑ Sibling 2 will give to the Primary Caregiver $ _____ per ❑week or ❑month toward Our Parent(s)' Routine Expenses:*
- ❑ Sibling 3 will give to the Primary Caregiver $ _____ per ❑week or ❑month toward Our Parent(s)' Routine Expenses:*
- ❑ Sibling 4 will give to the Primary Caregiver $ _____ per ❑week or ❑month toward Our Parent(s)' Routine Expenses:*

- ❑ until _____ (*date*).
- ❑ until otherwise agreed (_____).
- ❑ Siblings will follow the specific financial terms in Schedule C, "Our Parent(s)' Expenses."

*Routine Expenses are defined as daily expenses of food, lodging, clothes, ongoing prescription medications, toiletries, and ordinary transportation costs.

Major Expenses

- ❑ Siblings will consult each other regarding major expenses** before the money is spent.
- ❑ Once agreed on, Siblings agree to share Our Parent(s)' Major Expenses** ❑ equally or ❑ as follows: _____.
- ❑ And/or _____.

**Major expenses are defined as any expense over $ _____ not already included in this Agreement, such as plane fare, medical procedures or apparatus, home improvements, household maintenance, or home health care providers.

6. Major Decisions

If, in the event that Our Parent(s) is/are unable to make his/her/their own decisions and there are no legal directives, Siblings agree that:

Daily Decisions

- ❑ Daily decisions about the basic care for Our Parent(s) will lie with the Primary Caregiver.
- ❑ To the extent that Our Parent(s) is/are able, his/her/their wishes will be respected and will be given priority, as long as they fit within Siblings' abilities/resources.
- ❑ And/or _____.

Major Decisions

- ❑ Major Decisions[†] about Our Parent(s) will be left to the Primary Caregiver.
- ❑ Major Decisions[†] about Our Parent(s) will be made mutually, between Siblings.
- ❑ Major Decisions[†] about Our Parent(s) will be discussed between Siblings, but the Primary Caregiver has the final say, as it is his/her life that is impacted the most.
- ❑ And/or _____.

[†]Major Decisions are defined as those that involve the use and/or maintenance of the Parent(s)' property, medical and mental health care decisions, and any decision that will have a significant impact on the Parent(s) and/or one or more of the Siblings' financial or logistical obligations.

7. Communications

- ❑ Siblings will call the Primary Caregiver to discuss how Our Parent(s) is/are doing at these times: _____ *(For example: every Wednesday; twice a month, on the 1st and the 15th)*
- ❑ The Primary Caregiver is responsible for giving regular updates on Our Parent(s)' condition and general health every _____ *(month; week; two weeks)*.
- ❑ Siblings will inform each other of Our Parent(s)' urgent issues, medical needs, and emergencies, and/or anything unusual in Our Parent(s)' behavior and/or normal routines.
- ❑ And/or _____.

8. Additional Considerations

Due to the individuality of our family, Siblings(s) add the following considerations:

❑ _____
❑ _____
❑ _____

9. Signatures

A. We agree to take A Sane Approach to an Emotional Issue™. This Caring for Our Aging Parents Agreement reflects our understanding with regard to the caregiving of Our Parent(s). This Agreement replaces any previous agreements, oral or written, relating to caregiving of Our Parents.

Location where this Caring for Our Aging Parents Agreement is signed:

_____
CITY   STATE

Sibling 1: _____ ___/___/20___
PRINTED NAME   SIGNATURE   DATE

Sibling 2: _____ ___/___/20___
PRINTED NAME   SIGNATURE   DATE

Sibling 3: _____ ___/___/20___
PRINTED NAME   SIGNATURE   DATE

Sibling 4: _____ ___/___/20___
PRINTED NAME   SIGNATURE   DATE

INSTRUCTIONS:

1. Before signing, make a copy of the filled-in Agreement with any schedules and attachments.
2. Siblings sign both the original and the copies.
3. Siblings keep a signed copy. Include any signed attachments.

B. When the Caring for Our Aging Parents Agreement has ended, Siblings sign and date below on all copies of the Caring for Our Aging Parents Agreement documents.

THANK YOU. THE CARING FOR AGING PARENT AGREEMENT IS NOW ENDED.

Sibling 1's signature:_____ Date: ___/___/20 ___

Sibling 2's signature:_____ Date: ___/___/20 ___

Sibling 3's signature:_____ Date: ___/___/20 ___

Sibling 4's signature:_____ Date: ___/___/20 ___

Sharing Responsibilities

If applicable, define the Primary Caregiver. Fill out details when the Secondary Caregiver(s) will help with responsibilities for Our Parent(s).* Examples are given in italics.

SIBLING 1	SIBLING 2	SIBLING 3	SIBLING 4	RESPONSIBILITY	HOW OFTEN
		Primary Caregiver		*Overall*	*Daily*
	X			*Will drive our parent(s) to doctor's appointments*	*Weekly*

*Consider regular activities, such as meals, religious and other social activities, phone calls, and visits, as well as special events and activities, such as visiting on Sunday and taking Parent(s) for a stroll.

INITIAL & DATE

Sibling 1's initials: _____ Date: ___/___/20____

Sibling 2's initials: _____ Date: ___/___/20____

Sibling 3's initials: _____ Date: ___/___/20____

Sibling 4's initials: _____ Date: ___/___/20____

Rest for the Primary Caregiver and Visiting

Define the Primary Caregiver. Fill out details when the Secondary Caregiver(s) will help with Our Parent(s).* Examples are given in italics.

SIBLING 1	SIBLING 2	SIBLING 3	SIBLING 4	WHEN SECONDARY CAREGIVERS WILL VISIT AND/OR TAKE OVER THE CARE OF OUR PARENT(S)	FURTHER DETAILS**
		X		*Every Wednesday (start date __/__/20__)*	*Will take Our Parents grocery shopping*
				Summer Break (start date__/__/20__)	*Will pick up Our Parents and house them for 1 month*

* You know your family best, so customize this form to encompass your commitments.
** For example: When/where this will take place; how long; which days of the week.

INITIAL & DATE

Sibling 1's initials: _____ Date: ____/____/20____

Sibling 2's initials: _____ Date: ____/____/20____

Sibling 3's initials: _____ Date: ____/____/20____

Sibling 4's initials: _____ Date: ____/____/20____

Our Parent(s)' Expenses

Detail which sibling will pay, or what percentage each will contribute. Consider clothing, transportation, as well as extras, including gifts, subscriptions, and other specific expenses. You know your family best, so customize this form to encompass your commitment(s). Examples are given in italics.

SIBLING'S MONTHLY CONTRIBUTION	SIBLING 1		SIBLING 2		SIBLING 3		SIBLING 4		HOW OFTEN
ITEM	AMOUNT	%	AMOUNT	%	AMOUNT	%	AMOUNT	%	DAILY/WEEKLY/ MONTHLY/ANNUAL
			ROUTINE EXPENSES						
Groceries	*$150*	*100%*							
Medication	*$25*	*25%*	*$25*	*25%*	*$25*	*25%*	*$25*	*25%*	*Monthly*
			UNFORSEEN EXPENSES						
Church field trip		*50%*				*50%*			

INITIAL & DATE

Sibling 1's initials: _____ Date: ____/____/20____

Sibling 2's initials: _____ Date: ____/____/20____

Sibling 3's initials: _____ Date: ____/____/20____

Sibling 4's initials: _____ Date: ____/____/20____

Additional Siblings 5 through 7 Contact Information

If there are more than 3 siblings, fill out this form.

Sibling 5: _____
          FIRST   M.I.   LAST

Address: _____
         STREET   CITY   STATE   ZIP

Phone #: _____
         HOME   WORK   MOBILE

E-mail: _____

Sibling 6: _____
          FIRST   M.I.   LAST

Address: _____
         STREET   CITY   STATE   ZIP

Phone #: _____
         HOME   WORK   MOBILE

E-mail: _____

Sibling 7: _____
          FIRST   M.I.   LAST

Address: _____
         STREET   CITY   STATE   ZIP

Phone #: _____
         HOME   WORK   MOBILE

E-mail: _____

CHAPTER 9

Mom, Can I Have the Keys?

The Safe Driving Parent–Teen Driver Agreement

It happens before you know it. One minute you're pushing your child in a stroller and the next thing you know he's asking for the keys to the car. This monumental parenting moment marks a significant shift in control, and can put some parents into a panic. Parents are right to be concerned for their children. Driving requires reason, rationality, and maturity, none of which teenagers are known to have in great quantity.

They must obey the rules of the road. They have to drive defensively and watch out for others who might not be doing the right thing. They must make decisions about where they go and whom they go with, how fast to drive and what risks to take. One day they will have to decide not to drink and drive or not get into the car with someone who has been drinking.

You won't be there with them when the time for those choices arrives. They will have to make those decisions on their own. Worse yet, they may have to make them while they are with their friends and subjected to peer pressure. And while you have told them what they should and should not do, you are not sure they're really listening. After all, isn't it obligatory for them to roll their eyes at you at least three times a day? So what do you do to make sure they know how serious a responsibility driving is? How do you know they have heard you and understand what is required of them? Put it in writing.

Kelly's mom, Dianne, let Kelly use her car whenever she asked, but if Kelly took it out on a
Friday or Saturday night, Dianne would worry nonstop until the car and Kelly were safely back
in the driveway. She told Kelly again and again about the dangers of drunk driving. She even told

Kelly that if she was drinking she should just call home and Dianne would come and get her. But Kelly was afraid that Dianne would punish her by taking away the car if she did call.

Though it does not guarantee compliance, a Safe Driving Parent–Teen Driver Agreement sends a clear message about how serious driving is and how serious you are about the rules. Filling it out together requires you to go through your specific requirements. If you do not want your child driving friends around or lending the car to his buddies, you can spell that out. If you want the car returned clean and with a full tank of gas, you should write that down.

Jonah asked his dad, Brian, whether he could use the car to take "the boys" out to the Saturday night football game. The next morning, Brian found gum stuck to the floor mat, an orange soda stain on the passenger seat, as well as the distinctive smell of cigarette smoke lingering in the air inside the car. When he asked Jonah about it, Jonah said he had let his friend Marco take the car to pick up another friend during the halftime show. Brian didn't know if he was more annoyed about the mess or about Jonah lending out the car without permission.

The Safe Driving Parent–Teen Driver Agreement is a straightforward one. Note as well that it is very one-sided. It allows you, as parents, to set out rules for your new teen drivers. Even so, your children have no *right* to the car, nor do they have the *right* to drive. Remember that, as a parent, you have the right and responsibility to step in, if necessary. Your new driver should understand that not only must he obey the letter of the agreement but the spirit as well. At any point, if you do not like how things are going, you can and should take away the keys.

We ask for both parties to give their reasons for entering into the agreement at the beginning because it helps both of you understand why you want to have this agreement. This is a great time to have a conversation with your kid about the risks that come with driving a car and your reasons for being concerned.

You will want to go through all the Guidelines and Travel Limitations and Responsibilities with your teen. She might point out something you failed to consider but want to address, such as how she will get home from her job at the restaurant if she isn't supposed to be driving after midnight. Or if she will be allowed to drive outside the town limits when there is an "away" football game. You might consider being very restrictive at first and allow your teen more freedom (and a corresponding change in the agreement) if she demonstrates that she is responsible.

The Communication section reminds the teen that you expect to be kept in the loop and reminds him of the types of things that he has to tell you. Accidents can be scary, especially for a new driver, so an attachment is provided to keep in the car. It provides all the prompts your teen will need to record the important details, such as the other driver's insurance information and the names and contact information of witnesses.

Drew was driving his parents' SUV when he got into a little fender bender. The accident was so minor that the SUV was not damaged at all. The other man's car only had a small dent. Drew exchanged insurance information with him, but the man hardly seemed to care about the damage. In fact, he was very friendly. So Drew didn't bother telling his parents about the accident. No reason to upset them, he figured. But when the other driver's insurance company called Drew's parents several weeks later, his parents were furious. They didn't know a thing about an accident.

If the promise is broken, you have an opportunity to lay out certain conditions. Obeying all the driving rules may not be the only thing you want to make mandatory. Maintaining satisfactory grades, completing certain chores, or holding an after-school job can all be prerequisites for getting the keys. You may want to make it clear that if your teen comes home intoxicated or under the influence of a mind-altering substance of any kind, he will lose the right to use the car. Getting caught in a lie or suspended from school can be deal breakers, too. Explain to your child that loaning him a car requires trust, and any actions on his part that make you question your trust in him would be enough to revoke or restrict his privileges.

As a parent you have chosen to give your child an opportunity to drive. Remember that technical compliance with this agreement does not obligate you to give your new driver the keys to your car. Having an agreement in place does, however, give you some peace of mind when you do allow your child to drive, and it will set your child on the road to being a responsible, safe driver who knows what is expected of him.

Safe Driving Parent–Teen Driver

PAPER HANDSHAKE · PRINTED PROMISE · PUBLISHED COMMITMENT

The Parent(s) and the Teen Driver are making this Agreement because . . .

The Parent(s)' reasons: _____

_____

(For example: To support my child's independence as a Teen Driver; to rest assured that my child will make good judgments; to help my child to understand the responsibility that comes with driving)

The Teen Driver's reasons: _____

_____

(For example: To respect the family's driving parameters; to help my parents understand that I take driving seriously and that I'm going to obey the laws)

1. The Promise

Let's come together and respectfully sign this Agreement to ensure that everyone understands the responsibility that comes with driving. This document serves as an Agreement between Parents and their teenage Child about driving safely.

I/We, _____ *(Parent's name)* and _____ *(Parent's name),* agree(s) to be positive driving role model(s) and to provide support to the Teen Driver.

I, _____ *(Teen Driver's name),* agree to respect and obey all city, state, and federal driving laws, as well as to respect and obey driving privileges granted by my Parents, _____ *(Parent's name)* and _____ *(Parent's name).*

The Safe Driving Agreement begins: ___/___/20___.
The Safe Driving Agreement:

- ❏ Ends on ___/___/20___.
- ❏ Ends as soon as the Teen Driver turns 18 years old.
- ❏ Is always in effect, because we love each other.
- ❏ And/or _____.

2. Contact Information

Parent's/Guardian's name: _____
FIRST   M.I.   LAST   RELATIONSHIP

Address: _____
STREET   CITY   STATE   ZIP

Phone #: _____
HOME   WORK   MOBILE

E-mail: _____

Parent's/Guardian's name: _____
                                    FIRST   M.I.   LAST   RELATIONSHIP

Address: _____
        STREET   CITY   STATE   ZIP

Phone #: _____
          HOME   WORK   MOBILE

E-mail: _____

Teen Driver's name: _____
                       FIRST   M.I.   LAST   RELATIONSHIP

Address: _____
        STREET   CITY   STATE   ZIP

Phone #: _____
          HOME   WORK   MOBILE

E-mail: _____

Driver's Permit/License #: _____ State Issued: _____

3. Driving Guidelines

According to statistics, teenagers are more likely to be in a fatal crash than those in any other age group, and car crashes are more likely when someone else is in the car.

When it comes to driving, the Teen Driver agrees to the following:

❑ To always remain drug-free and sober.

❑ To stay away from anyone who isn't drug-free or sober and is operating, or about to operate, a motor vehicle.

❑ If the Teen Driver finds him/herself in a situation where there is no sober driver able to drive him/her home:

    ❑ The Teen Driver will call the Parent(s) to pick him/her up no matter where he/she is or what time it is.

    ❑ The Parent(s) promise to pick up the Teen Driver anywhere at any time the Teen Driver calls and says there is no responsible licensed sober person able to get him/her home.

    ❑ The Parent(s) will respect the Teen Driver's decision to call for a ride so highly that: _____
    _____.

    (For example: No questions will be asked; the Teen Driver won't be in any trouble; whatever trouble he/she will get in as a result of his/her behavior will be limited as follows, because the Teen Driver called)

    ❑ And/or _____.

❑ To always wear his/her seat belt, and require everyone else who is a passenger in his/her car to always wear a seat belt.

❑ To obey all traffic laws.

❑ To use a cell phone only when the car is stopped safely, on the side of the road, or in a parking lot.

❑ To keep the car smoke-free—no exceptions.

- ❏ To eat and drink only when the car is at a standstill.
- ❏ To call for a ride when feeling too tired or sick to drive.
- ❏ To refrain from driving if there is a bad storm, if roads are icy, or if it is snowing heavily.
- ❏ In case of an accident, the Teen Driver must report the accident and exchange insurance information with the other party involved. (The Teen Driver may tear out Attachment 1, "In Case of an Accident," and keep it in his/her glove compartment.)
- ❏ And/or _____.

4. Travel Limitations and Responsibility

According to statistics, driving between midnight and 5 a.m., and carrying passengers, drastically increases fatal car crashes for Teen Drivers.

The Teen Driver agrees*:

- ❏ To limit the number of passengers in his/her car to _____ people.
- ❏ To refrain from driving between the hours of _____ and _____, until _____. *(For example: The driver is more experienced; until he/she is 17, etc.)*
- ❏ To always stay within the city/town limits or _____ *(where),* unless the Teen Driver has specifically asked the Parent(s) for permission to do otherwise.
- ❏ To never let anyone else drive the car.
- ❏ And/or _____.

* Check state laws for legal limits.

When it comes to looking after and maintaining the car, the Teen Driver agrees:

- ❏ To make sure to routinely check the tire pressure and to keep track of oil changes.
- ❏ To pay for his/her own gas.
- ❏ To keep the car clean.
- ❏ To keep track of the keys and to always put them in the same spot when getting home so others can find them.
- ❏ To pay for his/her own insurance and to ensure that it's up-to-date.
- ❏ To contribute to insurance costs in the amount of $_____ per _____.
- ❏ And/or _____.

5. Communication

The Teen Driver Agrees:

- ❏ To ask the Parent(s)' permission each time the Teen Driver wishes to use the car.
- ❏ To notify the Parent(s) as to where the Teen Driver is going, whom the Teen Driver will be with, and when the Teen Driver is returning.
- ❏ To call the Parent(s) whenever the Teen Driver anticipates that the Teen Driver will be late.
- ❏ To notify the Parent(s) about any encounter with the police.
- ❏ Accidents happen! The Teen Driver will immediately notify the Parent(s) about any accident or fender bender. (If the Teen Driver is at fault, see consequences, below.)
- ❏ The Teen Driver and the Parent(s) will meet _____ *(monthly, every 3 months)* to discuss the Teen Driver's driving experiences and progress.

6. If the Promise Is Broken . . .

Although we do not anticipate any problems, we do think it is wise to include consequences in our Agreement, just in case something arises.

Traffic tickets:

❑ The Teen Driver will notify the Parent(s) as soon as possible if the Teen Driver receives a traffic ticket of any kind.

❑ The Teen Driver is responsible for paying for the ticket, and is responsible for any subsequent penalties.

❑ The Teen Driver will lose these driving privileges: _____ _____. *(For example: Driving his/her friends around; driving after dark)* until _____ _____ *(when).*

❑ And/or _____.

If the Teen Driver is involved in an accident:

❑ If the Teen Driver is at fault, the Teen Driver will be responsible for any ticket fee, court costs, insurance increases, or accident repair fees, and will follow through to take care of the situation.

❑ If the Teen Driver is at fault, the Teen Driver will lose these privileges: _____ _____ until _____ *(when).*

❑ And/or _____.

If the Teen Driver does not comply with our Agreement:

❑ The Teen Driver or the Parent(s) will receive a verbal reminder of the specific term(s) the Teen Driver or the Parent(s) is/are not honoring.

❑ The Teen Driver or the Parent(s) will be shown the specific terms, on our signed Agreement, which the Teen Driver or the Parent(s) is/are not honoring.

❑ The Teen Driver will lose the privilege of driving.

❑ And/or _____.

If the Teen Driver drives in an intoxicated state, or drives with someone else who is in an intoxicated state:

❑ The Teen Driver will lose all driving privileges for a period of _____.

❑ The Teen Driver will suffer the following consequences:_____ _____.

7. Additional Family Considerations

Due to the individuality of our family, the Parent(s) add the following considerations:

❑ _____.

❑ _____.

❑ _____.

The Teen Driver adds the following considerations:

❑ _____.

❑ _____.

❑ _____.

❑ _____.

8. Signatures

A. We agree to take A Sane Approach to an Emotional Issue™. This is a serious Agreement and we understand and agree to the terms. Upon signing, the Teen Driver is welcome to start driving.

Agreed to and signed by:

The Parent: _____ ___/___/20___
                     PRINTED NAME   SIGNATURE   DATE

The Parent: _____ ___/___/20___
                     PRINTED NAME   SIGNATURE   DATE

The Teen Driver: _____ ___/___/20___
                     PRINTED NAME   SIGNATURE   DATE

INSTRUCTIONS:

1. Before signing, make a copy of the filled-in Agreement.
2. The Teen Driver and the Parent(s) sign both the original and the copy.
3. The Teen Driver and the Parent(s) both keep a signed copy.

B. When the Parent(s) and the Teen Driver's Agreement has ended, both parties sign and date below on both documents: the Teen Driver's document and the Parent(s)' document.

THANK YOU. THE SAFE DRIVING PARENT–TEEN DRIVER AGREEMENT IS NOW ENDED.

Parent's signature:_____ Date: ___/___/20 ___

Parent's signature:_____ Date: ___/___/20 ___

Teen Driver's signature:_____ Date: ___/___/20 ___

Attachment 1: In Case of an Accident*

ITEM	ENTER DETAILS BELOW
Accident Information	
Date of accident:	
Location of accident:	
City/town:	
County:	
State:	
Police Department involved:	
Accident report #:	
Police officer on scene:	
Police officer's badge #:	
Driver's Information	
Name of driver:	
Address:	
Phone #:	
Year/make/model of motor vehicle:	
License plate #:	
Other Party's Information	
Name of driver:	
Address of driver:	
Phone # of driver:	
Name of registered owner of motor vehicle:	
Address of registered owner of motor vehicle:	
Phone # of registered owner of motor vehicle:	
Year/make/model of motor vehicle:	

ITEM	ENTER DETAILS BELOW
License plate #:	
Insurance company name:	
Insurance company policy #:	
Witness(es)	
Name:	
Address:	
Phone #:	
Name:	
Address:	
Phone #:	

*Keep this Attachment in the glove compartment in case of an accident.

CHAPTER 10

Move Over, Rover!

The Shared Pet/Pet Parenting Agreement

Sharing your home with a pet can be one of life's greatest joys. For some people, life without a furry or feathered companion is unimaginable. These creatures bring unconditional love, companionship, fun, and adventure. And work! If you and your roommate or friend decide you want to adopt a pet, you'd better be ready to take on the responsibility. Together. And writing down a plan for how you will do that can make the whole thing less hairy!

The Shared Pet/Pet Parenting Agreement can be modified for a parent to use with a child who wants to adopt a pet. Almost every parent has heard the plea, "I'll walk and feed him myself and you won't have to do anything. I promise!" With this agreement the child can put his promise in writing. Obviously, the child can't really manage all the care for an animal on his own so, at a minimum, the parent needs to be prepared for the financial obligation and to take the pet to the vet or for grooming.

Consider realistically what you are ready and willing to take on before you commit to pet ownership. Any type of pet will require care, but some require more than others. If you both love dogs and want to get one, be prepared to feed and walk your canine two or three times a day. If you get a puppy, he has to be housebroken and trained. You can't pick up and go away for the weekend without making arrangements for your dog's care. If both pet parents work long hours, you may need to trade off who will come home to walk the dog at lunch or find a neighbor who can walk him. He will need regular visits to the vet, along with vaccinations. The list of things you need to do for a dog is much longer than, say, the list for fish. You can expect that your emotional attachment will be more significant, too.

A new trend in pet ownership is shared ownership between people living separately. By doing this, people can experience the joy and companionship of a pet without the full-time commitment and the full financial burden. It is ideal for people who travel frequently or have erratic work schedules. If you are considering an arrangement like this, you will find the Shared Pet/Pet Parenting Agreement is especially helpful. Each one of you can specify what you will contribute and how much time you plan to spend with your animal.

Carmella always loved dogs but she couldn't have one because of her demanding work schedule. She was an actress and when she was in a show, she could be away from home as long as fifteen hours each day. And sometimes she had to go on the road for several weeks at a time. But when she wasn't in a show, Carmella had all day to pine for an animal companion. Her neighbors, the Perez family, had three kids, and though the kids would love a dog of their own, the parents felt that five people and a dog would be too chaotic in their two-bedroom apartment. So the two families decided to adopt a dog together. The dog could live in Carmella's apartment primarily, but would spend several hours each day at the Perezes' home and would be welcome there whenever Carmella traveled.

If you are living with someone, you should talk your decision through together before you leap in. The classic story of a boyfriend surprising his girlfriend with a puppy doesn't always end well. Both people may fall in love with the dog—but out of love with each other. You may decide that it makes more sense for one person to adopt and take full responsibility for the pet. Or you may want to split the costs and caregiving duties in half. You may realize that hamsters better suit your lifestyles and that a puppy would be too much work. The timing might not be right to take in the adorable stray kittens your cousin told you about. As roommates, you need to discuss these things so that both of you know what you are getting involved in and what to expect down the road. The Shared Pet/Pet Parenting Agreement will help you work through these considerations.

When he moved out of his family home, Mark really wanted to get a dog. His new roommate, Calvin, wasn't interested but said that if Mark took care of it, he didn't mind having a dog around. So Mark brought home an adorable Rottweiler puppy. For the first few weeks, things were great. Calvin even grew to like Spike and would occasionally take him to the park or toss the ball for him in the yard. But when Mark went on business trips, Calvin found himself fully responsible for taking care of the 75-pound Spike—a dog he didn't really want in the first place! And Mark apparently didn't think a thing of it.

You will need to identify your pet in the agreement. This may sound unwarranted, since, in your opinion, nobody could mistake your lizard Fifi's big brown eyes. But take the time to describe the pet as thoroughly as possible. If a person isn't familiar with lizards, Fifi's eyes probably look like any other reptile's. List the pet's name, breed, color, height, weight, gender, markings, and any other specifics that help identify the pet. You might take photos or a video to attach to the document so that anyone would recognize your pet. If the pet has a license or registration, or if there is a receipt or other relevant documentation, be sure to copy it and attach it to your agreement as well. You should use the Pet Identification Record attachment so that the most important information regarding the pet is in one place.

Since disagreements or squabbles can come up when one person or the other thinks she is doing more than her share, the Shared Pet/Pet Parenting Agreement allows you to get very specific about who will be doing what. Will one roommate handle all the vet and grooming appointments while the other takes care of walking and cleaning up after the pet? Can one person take care of all morning duties and the other cover the afternoon, evening, and weekends? Will expenses be split evenly?

You'll want to establish regular communication about your pet so that you can both be sure the arrangement is working out for you and for your pet. This is especially important if the people sharing the pet live separately and the pet has two homes. In addition, when you sign, you will be agreeing to keep the other pet parent informed of any appointments, changes in schedule, behavioral or health concerns, or any other pet-related issues.

Here are a few things to think about if one person does not keep his commitment to you and your shared pet. Remember that the agreement is meant to establish clear communication so your first step will always be to discuss the terms of the agreement, specifically the area that is in question, in hopes of clearing up any misunderstanding. If one person still doesn't comply after a reminder, that person might lose the privilege of sharing the pet or incur another consequence you deem appropriate.

If you are a parent using the agreement with a child, you'll need to be careful about the consequences, since you can't very well unadopt a pet if things aren't working out. More realistic perhaps is to take away other privileges, like TV or computer time, if the child isn't holding up her end of the bargain. Or, if the pet has a short life span, you can decide not to get another.

The agreement notes when the pet sharing arrangement begins and ends. You can indicate a specific date, or the duration of the shared residence, or for the life of the pet.

Michelle and Louise both loved cats, so the first thing they did after moving into their shared apartment was to go to the shelter and adopt a brother and sister pair of kittens. The kitties couldn't have been cuter, and they played so nicely together. Unfortunately, the same couldn't be said of Michelle and Louise. They didn't get along very well at all and after a year Michelle decided to move out. It would be unthinkable to separate the cats, and both girls wanted to keep the pair. It was clear they hadn't thought this through.

Keep in mind that the life span of your chosen pet and the duration of your cohabitation may not coincide. Dogs and cats, for instance, live ten years or more. A Scarlet Macaw parrot can live fifty years or more. How likely is it that your living arrangements will remain the same for that long? In your agreement you can establish what will happen to your pet when one pet parent moves on. There is even a place for you to spell out responsibilities if you both want to stay involved with the pet even though you live apart.

Sharing a pet is a testament to a strong relationship between two people. They have decided that together they can work out everything involved in taking care of an animal. A Shared Pet/Pet Parenting Agreement becomes a tool to keep your relationship and your animal healthy.

Shared Pet/Pet Parenting

PAPER HANDSHAKE • PRINTED PROMISE • PUBLISHED COMMITMENT

The Pet Parents are making this Agreement because . . .

Pet Parent A's reasons: _____

_____

Pet Parent B's reasons: _____

_____

(For example: To enjoy the companionship of a pet and to share the responsibilities; I can't be a full-time owner; the Pet was given as a present to be shared between us; it's our first family pet; to teach my child pet-caring responsibilities)

I. The Promise

Let's come together and respectfully sign this Agreement to ensure that everyone understands the responsibility and the joy of owning a pet. This document serves as an Agreement between both Pet Parents about sharing and caring for Our Pet.

As Pet Parents we, _____ (Pet Parent A's name) and _____ *(Pet Parent B's name)*, together agree to love and take care of Our Pet, _____ *(Pet's name)*, and be respectful of one another and follow through on our commitment to Our Pet.

Pet Parent A is the: ❏ Sole Owner of the Pet or ❏ a Co-owner of the Pet or ❏ a Non-owner of the Pet

Pet Parent B is the: ❏ Sole Owner of the Pet or ❏ a Co-owner of the Pet or ❏ a Non-owner of the Pet

Describe your Pet:

_____

_____

(For example: 3-year-old male Siamese cat, blue eyes, black face; 6-month-old pug, light brown, tattooed in ear; 2-year-old Macaw parrot, red and green coloring, named Nippy for a reason)

❏   See Attachment 1 and complete "Pet Identification Record."

The Pet Parenting Agreement begins: ___/___/20___

The Pet Parenting Agreement ends:

❏   On ___/___/20___

❏   On the day we stop sharing the same home.

❏   On the day we dissolve this Agreement.

❏   With the death of the Pet.

❏   And/or _____.

2. Contact Information

Pet Parent A Name: _____
FIRST   M.I.   LAST   RELATIONSHIP TO OTHER PET PARENT

Address: _____
STREET   CITY   STATE   ZIP

Phone #:_____
HOME   WORK   MOBILE

E-mail: _____

Pet Parent B Name: _____
FIRST   M.I.   LAST   RELATIONSHIP TO OTHER PET PARENT

Address: _____
STREET   CITY   STATE   ZIP

Phone #:_____
HOME   WORK   MOBILE

E-mail: _____

3. Health Care and Responsibilities

Our Pet is very important to us and so are its health and care:

❑ The Sole Owner Pet Parent will be responsible for all health and caregiving responsibilities.

❑ Pet Parents will share responsibilities. (See Schedule A, "Pet Care Responsibilities and Expenses" to indicate responsibilities in further detail.)

Or:

Pet Parents agree to be consistent about the following guidelines:

❑ Our Pet's feeding schedule is as follows: _____

❑ Our Pet's exercise schedule is as follows: _____

❑ Our Pet takes his/her medicine as follows: _____

❑ Regarding table scraps, we agree that: _____

❑ Regarding discipline, we agree that: _____

❑ Our Pet is only to sleep: _____

❑ Pet Parent who has the Pet under his/her care is responsible for any damages caused by the Pet.

4. Finances and Shared Expenses

❑ The Sole Owner Pet Parent will pay all Pet expenses.

❑ Pet Parents will share Pet expenses in the following percentages:

❑ Pet Parent A _____%; ❑ Pet Parent B _____%.

❑ Any expenses over $_____ will be discussed and agreed on by Pet Parents before the money is spent.

❑ The cost of a rental-residence security deposit specifically for Pet(s) will be shared:

❑ Pet Parent A _____%; ❑ Pet Parent B _____%.

- ❑ Pet Parents are responsible for keeping records of their expenditures.
- ❑ And/or _____.
- ❑ See Schedule A, "Pet Care Responsibilities and Expenses," to specify how much each Pet Parent pays, and for which expenses.

5. If/When Pet Parents Stop Sharing the Same Residence (Or Want to End This Agreement)

Pet Parents agree that the Pet will live with:

- ❑ The Sole Owner Pet Parent
- ❑ Pet Parent A or ❑ Pet Parent B or ❑ alternately between both Pet Co-Owners.
- ❑ And/or _____.

6. Communication

Pet Parents agree to notify each other in a timely manner:

- ❑ About the Pet's appointments.
- ❑ When the Pet Parent needs to make a change in the Pet care schedule.
- ❑ If the Pet becomes ill or is behaving strangely.
- ❑ And/or _____.

7. Additional Considerations

Due to the individuality of our Pet Sharing, we add the following considerations:

Pet Parent A:

- ❑ _____
- ❑ _____
- ❑ _____
- ❑ _____
- ❑ _____

Pet Parent B:

- ❑ _____
- ❑ _____
- ❑ _____
- ❑ _____
- ❑ _____

8. If the Promise Is Broken

- ❑ Pet Parent will receive a verbal reminder of the specific terms that he/she is not honoring.
- ❑ Pet Parent could lose the right to share the Pet.
- ❑ Pet Parents may collectively have to find the Pet a new home.
- ❑ And/or _____
_____.

9. In the Event of the Death of the Sole Owner Pet Parent

For these intentions to be formally and legally recognized, they must be entered into a valid will.

❑ The Pet goes to the surviving Pet Parent.

❑ See Attachment 2, "In the Event of the Death of the Sole Owner Pet Parent."

10. Signatures

A. We agree to take A Sane Approach to an Emotional Issue™. This Shared Pet/Pet Parenting Agreement reflects our understanding with regard to sharing the Pet. This Agreement replaces any previous agreements, oral or written, relating to the Pet.

Location where Shared Pet/Pet Parenting Agreement is signed:

_____
CITY   STATE

Pet Parent A: _____ ___/___/20___
              PRINTED NAME   SIGNATURE   DATE

Pet Parent B: _____ ___/___/20___
              PRINTED NAME   SIGNATURE   DATE

INSTRUCTIONS:

1. Before signing, make a copy of the filled-in Agreement with schedules and attachment.
2. Pet Parent A and Pet Parent B sign both the original and the copy.
3. Pet Parent A and Pet Parent B both keep a signed copy.

B. When the Shared Pet/Pet Parenting Agreement has ended, Pet Parent A and Pet Parent B sign and date below on both Shared Pet/Pet Parent Agreement documents; Pet Parent A's document, and Pet Parent B's document.

THANK YOU. THE SHARED PET/PET PARENTING AGREEMENT IS NOW ENDED.

Pet Parent A's signature:_____ Date: ___/___/20 ___

Pet Parent B's signature:_____ Date: ___/___/20 ___

Pet Care Responsibilities and Expenses

PET CARE RESPONSIBILITIES

Each Pet Parent will complete each caregiving responsibility:

CARE AND WELFARE OF PET	PET PARENT A	PET PARENT B	HOW OFTEN AND/OR WHEN

Examples: Feed and water, buy pet supplies, provide medical care, exercise daily, wash and groom, clean up poop.

EXPENSE PAYMENTS

Each Pet Parent contributes to Pet Expenses as follows:

EXPENSE	PET PARENT A PAYS	%	PET PARENT B PAYS	%

Examples: Pet food, supplies, grooming, vet bills, pet travel, kennel, pet sitting, insurance, training.

INITIAL & DATE

Pet Parent A initials: _____ Date: ____/____/20____

Pet Parent B initials: _____ Date: ____/____/20____

Pet Identification Record

Contact Information:

Pet Parent A's name:_____ Date: ___/___/20 ___

Pet Parent B's name:_____ Date: ___/___/20 ___

Pet's name: _____

Pet's breed: _____

Pet's description/special characteristics: _____

Pet's breeder   Name: _____

                  Address: _____

                  Phone #: _____

Pet adoption/purchased from and date: _____

Pet's license #: _____

Pet's chip #: _____

Pet's birthdate: _____

Pet's vet   Name: _____

           Address: _____

           Phone #: _____

Pet's special diet: _____

Pet's other special needs: _____

Photograph and/or video of Pet attached
(include most current documentation with date) _____

In the Event of the Death of the Sole Owner Pet Parent

In the event of the Sole Pet Owner's death, the Pet will go to the following designated individual:

Name: _____
           FIRST   M.I.   LAST

For these intentions to be formally and legally recognized, they must be entered into a valid will.

THE SOLE PET OWNER'S REPRESENTATIVE'S CONTACT INFORMATION

Sole Pet Owner's Representative

Name: _____
           FIRST   M.I.   LAST   TITLE

Relationship to Sole Pet Owner: _____

(For example: Attorney, brother or sister, parent)

Address: _____
           STREET   CITY   STATE   ZIP

Phone #:_____
           HOME   WORK   MOBILE

E-mail: _____

INITIAL & DATE

Pet Parent A's initials: _____ Date: ____/____/20____

Pet Parent B's initials: _____ Date: ____/____/20____

The Witness' initials (if wanted): _____ Date: ____/____/20____

CHAPTER 11

My Home Is Your Home

The Lending Your Vacation Home Agreement

A vacation home is great to own and even better to borrow. It is located in a pleasant place and stays empty much of the time. For owners, lending or renting your home can be a great way to help cover the costs and have occupants look after your place. For borrowers or renters, staying in a friend's vacation home can be more comfortable and affordable than a standard hotel room. Benefits notwithstanding, borrowing or lending a vacation home can become a source of aggravation. The best way to make sure such an arrangement works to everyone's advantage is to discuss specifics in advance and then write them down!

Typically, when vacation home owners rent to strangers they insist on a lease agreement. But many owners don't want strangers using their place and prefer to keep it for themselves, their families, and their friends. Still, they should document the exchange and spell out everyone's expectations.

The Crowleys and the Watsons had been friends for years, so when the Crowleys asked to use the Watsons' Florida condo for a month, the Watsons didn't see a problem. Unfortunately, when the Watsons returned to their vacation home weeks after the Crowleys had used it, they found a huge unpaid electric bill and water damage to the ceiling in the living room below the master bath. When Mrs. Watson called Mrs. Crowley, an argument ensued. Mrs. Crowley said, quite truthfully, that they had never told the Watsons that they would pay for the utilities while they were there. And as for water damage? They knew nothing about it.

It is easy to see how a misunderstanding would arise. And how a simple Lending Your

Vacation Home Agreement would have helped the Crowleys and the Watsons keep their friendship strong. The Watsons would have let the Crowleys know about the electric bill and the Crowleys would have noted that the condition of the condo was fine when they left.

As in other agreements, it is smart to note up front why the owner and the borrower are making these arrangements. Each one of you should state your reasons so both sides are sure what to expect. If a borrower says that she is looking for accommodations large enough for her whole family, that will alert the owner to the number of people she expects to stay at the home. If an owner wants to be sure his house is occupied during the off season for added security, saying so will let the borrower know that he expects her to be visible to the neighbors.

The basic promise of the agreement is where you answer all the preliminary questions. What property will be loaned and how long is the loan for? It also lays out any financial arrangements. That can be the hardest thing to bring up verbally, especially between friends. Filling out this agreement will require you to address this issue without having to discuss it separately. Oftentimes, friends will decide not to exchange money but will make some other equally beneficial arrangement. Perhaps the borrowers have offered to loan their own house in a different vacation spot, or they may barter services. These options should come up as part of the discussion.

> The Mitchells lent out their vacation home to their best friends' adult daughter, Jo-Anna, when Jo-Anna was going through a painful divorce. Though she couldn't afford rent, Jo-Anna wanted to pay something in return for their kind favor. Jo-Anna was a budding artist—and Betty Mitchell was looking for new art for her vacation home. Jo-Anna offered to paint two large canvases in specific colors for the Mitchells' living room and master bedroom, in lieu of rent. Not only did the work help Jo-Anna to heal emotionally, but it also bolstered her artist's resume. And after people saw Jo-Anna's work displayed in the Mitchells' vacation home, she received two other jobs from the Mitchells' well-to-do friends, which launched her now-successful career as a professional artist.

If you are the homeowner, take time to think things through. You may be happy enough to lend your house, but haven't considered the costs associated with running it. Do you want to be out of pocket for anything incurred while the borrowers are there? What do your utilities normally cost when the house is unoccupied? Do you want the borrower to pay the whole bill or just the difference? Are there fees if the borrowers use certain resort amenities? Do you want them to pay to have the house professionally cleaned upon their departure?

In your agreement you will also address what the borrowers should do if something breaks during their occupancy. You have to determine who is responsible. Having the condition of the property well documented will help make this easier, but all parties should be clear up front about what they need to do if some major expense is involved.

Both the owner and the borrower should be explicit about what the borrower can and cannot do. The Limitations on Use section will help you with this. Can the borrowers use the golf cart, boat, or snowmobile? Can they have parties or sleepover guests? Should they be able to make any small repairs or alterations on the property without your permission, like replacing the screen on the door if it has holes in it? Can they use the firewood stacked next to the house?

Miguel and Soledad thought they had covered everything when they told their friends, the DeGuzmans, that they could stay in their beach house. They had spent time politely laying down the guidelines over the phone: to please not use the speedboat, as it was in need of repair, and to please leave things as they were when they found them. The DeGuzmans seemed happy to oblige. However, the DeGuzmans had failed to mention that their two dogs accompanied them when they traveled. When Miguel and Soledad arrived at their beach house after the DeGuzmans had left, they found a distinctive doggy odor permeating their bedroom and living room, and black dog hair on the white couch and comforters. It wouldn't have been so bad had Soledad not been terribly allergic to dog hair.

Home security must be addressed as well. This may seem like common sense, but it's better to bring everything up in advance, especially if you have an alarm system or specific concerns. Some people don't think it is necessary to lock doors in the wilderness or they may not realize that the beachfront is open to the public and the gate to the pool needs to be kept closed to discourage trespassing. As the owner, you should make the borrowers aware of your security measures.

Take special note of the attachment to this agreement. You will want to pay close attention when describing the condition of the property. If the rug has a few stains, note that so the borrowers don't have to worry that they will be blamed for causing those stains. You should consider including photos or a video so that everyone is clear about the state of the property when it changes occupancy. This would have helped the Crowleys and the Watsons a great deal, and you will find that it will help you, too.

There is an additional and optional attachment where owners can list some of their favorite activities, restaurants, and area attractions. Sometimes the very best part of sharing a vacation house is sharing the insider secrets that make the spot special. Including this type of information will help foster the spirit of friendship that lies at the heart of the agreement.

Lending Your Vacation Home

PAPER HANDSHAKE · PRINTED PROMISE · PUBLISHED COMMITMENT

We are making this Agreement because . . .

The Owner's reason(s): _____

_____

_____

(For example: To give someone a gift; to provide an introduction to the area; because The Borrower has asked; to lend for a charity event; to promote our vacation home)

The Borrower's reason(s): _____

_____

_____

(For example: The Owner has offered to lend the property; to have a great vacation while saving money; to see a new town or country)

1. The Promise

The Owner invites the Borrower to be a welcomed guest and enjoy his/her/our Vacation Home. This document serves as a Lending Your Vacation Home Agreement between both of us, the Owner and the Borrower, in order to secure the dates of occupation and enjoyment of the Vacation Home.

As Owner, I, _____ *(Owner's name)*, agree ❏ to lend ❏ to rent to the Borrower my Vacation Home located at the following address: _____.

And I, _____ *(Borrower's name)*, agree to enjoy and respect the use of the Owner's Vacation Home during my vacation stay.

Description of the Vacation Home: _____

_____

_____

(For example: A two-level, Craftsman-style house on beachfront property; a two-bedroom log cabin on ten forested acres; a one-bedroom, one-bathroom apartment on the Upper East Side of Manhattan)

See Attachment 1, "Photographic Documentation Record," to identify the Property in further detail.

The Borrower's arrival date is: ___/___/20___; check-in time after___ a.m. or ___ p.m.

The Borrower's departure date is:

❏   ___/___/20___; check-out time before _____ a.m. or _____ p.m.

❏   And/or _____.

2. Contact Information

The Owner's name: _____
                         FIRST   M.I.   LAST   RELATIONSHIP TO BORROWER

Address: _____
        STREET   CITY   STATE   ZIP

Phone #:_____
        HOME   WORK   MOBILE

E-mail: _____

Property Manager and/or Management Company:

_____
    FIRST   M.I.   LAST   TITLE

Address: _____
        STREET   CITY   STATE   ZIP

Phone #:_____
        HOME   WORK   MOBILE

E-mail: _____

The Borrower's name: _____
                          FIRST   M.I.   LAST   RELATIONSHIP TO OWNER

Address: _____
        STREET   CITY   STATE   ZIP

Phone #:_____
        HOME   WORK   MOBILE

E-mail: _____

3. Security Deposit

The Owner agrees that the Borrower:

❑ Is welcome to stay in the Vacation Home free of charge; no rent is due.

❑ Is welcome to stay in the Vacation Home rent-free, but the Borrower will be charged for_____(*telephone, electric, water etc.*) used during the vacation stay.

❑ Will pay rent in the amount of $_____.

❑ Will pay a nonrefundable deposit of $_____ to secure the dates above with this signed Agreement delivered to the Owner. The other _____%, the balance of rent, will be paid _____ days prior to the first day of the rental term.

❑ Can use bartered forms of payment, in place of rent, such as: _____.
(*For example: Painting the house; yard work; creating a sculpture for the property*)

    ❑ See Schedule A "Bartered Rent Payment in Place of Monetary Payment," for a more detailed description and schedule.

❑ And/or _____.

Security/Damage Deposit:

- ❏ The Borrower will provide a security deposit in the amount of $_____ .
    - ❏ The security deposit will be due on_____ .
    - ❏ The security deposit will be returned to the borrower upon:
        - ❏ Owner verifying the condition of the property within___days of the Borrower's departure.
        - ❏ Return of Vacation Home keys.
        - ❏ And/or _____.
    - ❏ Owner will deduct amounts from the deposit to cover costs of any damage (other than normal wear and tear) done to the premises or expenses incurred by the Borrower for which the Borrower is responsible under this agreement.
    - ❏ And/or _____.
    - ❏ See Attachment 1, "Photographic Documentation Record," to identify the Property in further detail.

4. Limitations on Use of the Vacation Home

The Owner places these limitations on the use of the Property: _____

_____

_____

(For example: You may not alter the home physically; you may not have a party for more than 10 people; you may not use the powerboat; you may not drink the wine from the wine cellar; pets are not allowed)

5. Care and Maintenance

The Borrower will:

- ❏ Take good care of the Vacation Home.
- ❏ Not make any alterations to the Vacation Home.
- ❏ Accept responsibility/liability caused by a family member or guest of the Borrower who does not live up to the Lending Your Vacation Home Agreement.
- ❏ Never leave the Property unsecured when unattended.
- ❏ Use the home alarm system whenever he/she/they are leaving it unattended.
- ❏ Keep doors and windows closed and locked when leaving.
- ❏ Notify the Owner immediately of any major mechanical malfunctions.
- ❏ And/or _____.

6. Communication

The Owner and the Borrower agree:

- ❏ Any questions that the Borrower may have concerning the Vacation Home shall be directed to _____ at _____.
- ❏ The Owner has the right to show the Vacation Home to prospective clients ❏ with 24 hours' notice to the Borrower ❏ at the Borrower's convenience.
- ❏ The Owner has right to inspect the premises at any time if the Owner has reasonable cause to believe the Borrower or any person is misusing or damaging the Vacation Home or furnishings inside.
- ❏ And/or _____.

7. Additional Considerations

Due to the individuality of our Agreement, we add the following considerations:

The Owner:

❑ _____

❑ _____

❑ _____

❑ See Attachment 2, "Vacation Home Favorite Activities."

The Borrower:

❑ _____

❑ _____

❑ _____

8. Signatures

A. We agree to take A Sane Approach to an Emotional Issue™. This Lending Your Vacation Home Agreement reflects our understanding regarding the use of the Vacation Home by the Borrower. This Agreement replaces any previous agreements, oral or written, relating to the Vacation Home.

Location where this Agreement is signed:

_____
CITY   STATE

The Owner: _____ ___/___/20___
                    PRINTED NAME   SIGNATURE   DATE

The Borrower: _____ ___/___/20___
                    PRINTED NAME   SIGNATURE   DATE

Witness (if wanted): _____ ___/___/20___
                    PRINTED NAME   SIGNATURE   DATE

INSTRUCTIONS:

1. Before signing, make a copy of the filled-in Agreement with schedules and attachment.
2. The Owner and the Borrower sign both the original and the copy.
3. The Owner and the Borrower both keep a signed copy.

B. When the Lending Your Vacation Home Agreement has ended, the Borrower and the Owner sign and date below on both documents: the Borrower's document and the Owner's document.

THANK YOU. THE LENDING YOUR VACATION HOME AGREEMENT IS NOW ENDED.

The Owner's signature:_____ Date: ___/___/20 ___

The Borrow's signature:_____ Date: ___/___/20 ___

Bartered Rent Payment in Place of Monetary Rent Payment

In Place of Rent, the Borrower agrees to do the following:

WORK OR TRADE	DETAILS	TO BE COMPLETED (MONTH/DAY/YEAR)	SIGNED OFF ON (DATE AND INITIAL)

INITIAL & DATE

The Owner's initials: _____ Date: ___/___/20___

The Borrower's initials: _____ Date: ___/___/20___

Photographic Documentation Record

Photographic and/or Additional Descriptions

Describe the Vacation Property in further detail:

_____

_____

_____

_____

_____

_____

_____

_____

_____

_____

_____

_____

_____

_____

Attach any additional documentation:

❑ Current photograph(s) of the Vacation Home (initial and date).

❑ Current video of the Vacation Home (initial and date).

❑ Further documentation (such as purchase receipt[s]): _____

_____

_____

_____

_____

❑ And/or _____.

INITIAL & DATE

The Owner's initials: _____ Date: ____/____/20____

The Borrower's initials: _____ Date: ____/____/20____

Vacation Home Favorite Activities

FAVORITE RESTAURANTS

NAME & TYPE OF CUISINE	ADDRESS	PHONE NUMBER

INTERESTING SITES TO SEE

NAME OF SITE	COMMENTS	ADDITIONAL INFORMATION

ACTIVITIES

DESCRIPTION OF ACTIVITY	ADDRESS	PHONE NUMBER

OTHER "MUSTS"

DESCRIPTION	ADDRESS	PHONE NUMBER

CHAPTER 12

Just Between Us

The Personal Confidentiality Agreement

"Shhhh." "Don't tell anyone." "It's a secret." For as long as we've been talking, we have been keeping secrets (and not keeping them!). "I promise I won't tell a soul" only goes so far. It seems as if someone always takes it upon himself to share supposedly confidential information, either maliciously or innocently. Of course, the blabber then swears the person he tells to secrecy. After all, it *is* a secret.

When we have information that we really need to guard, we should have more than someone's word. We should have his printed promise. Asking him to sign an agreement sends that person a very clear and deliberate message about just how serious we are about privacy. And it gives us some recourse should our confidential information find its way into the public domain.

The Personal Confidentiality Agreement can be useful for personal situations like a pregnancy, a lottery win, an illness, or cosmetic surgery. We often need advice or additional assistance, but are afraid to ask for it because of our need to keep something secret. Drafting a Personal Confidentiality Agreement allows for limited disclosure while protecting both parties.

When Robert won the lottery, he was ecstatic but also nervous. He'd heard stories of winners losing friends and family over the money. He became suspicious of everyone around him. Before he told anyone about his winning ticket, he wanted to talk to his cousin, who was an accountant. But how could he be sure that she wouldn't spill the beans?

The first step in drafting this agreement is to identify the information that is to be kept confidential. The owner of the information, or the person with the secret, needs to specify exactly what it is that should be kept between the parties, or the "confider" and the "confidant." For instance, if someone is seeking advice from a family member because she is ill, she may want to be sure the other person will keep the specific diagnosis between them, but also won't disclose any aspect of her visits to the doctor, upcoming procedures, or her prognosis. She can specify this in writing.

In this agreement, each of you is asked to identify your goals in sharing the information. Doing this makes the purpose of the agreement clear, and each of you will recognize why you are involved.

Both of you will also identify acceptable means of passing information between you—in person? in writing? by e-mail? by phone? Depending on the nature of the information, you may want to be very specific here.

Kate was so excited after reading her friend Anna's manuscript that she sent her an e-mail at work to tell her how terrific she thought the book would be. When Anna's boss saw the e-mail, he was not happy to learn that she was writing about the company. Anna hadn't thought to tell Kate that her boss often worked on her computer.

Because of the private and personal nature of this agreement—and of the information itself—you may want to specify how you would like to secure it. Do you think it is necessary to use a safe deposit box or is keeping it in a private desk drawer acceptable? Would you be devastated if your best friend's husband found a copy of your agreement, complete with the secret information, in his wife's nightstand? You should consider how many snoops may be able to access it and how carefully you feel the information should be guarded.

It is hard to keep track of information sharing, but the agreement should also address what will happen if the information is leaked. Will the confidant lose particular privileges? Will there be financial consequences? Are there legal consequences if a copyright is breached?

Finally, the confider should lay out her expectation for when, if ever, and how the information can be shared publicly. It may also be necessary to define how each party should destroy the information.

With a Personal Confidentiality Agreement in hand, the confider or the owner of the information can feel assured that the trusted parties will guard the information, and the trusted parties will appreciate the responsibility that comes with keeping information to themselves.

Personal Confidentiality

PAPER HANDSHAKE · PRINTED PROMISE · PUBLISHED COMMITMENT

The Confider and the Confidant are making this Agreement because . . .

The Confider's reason(s): _____

_____

_____

(For example: To share a secret and ensure that it will be kept a secret; to feel relief in sharing this very delicate information with someone else)

The Confidant's reason(s): _____

_____

(For example: To assure the Confider that I can be trusted; to create a trusting atmosphere with my friend and support him/her through this time in the way that he/she needs me)

I. The Promise

I, the Confider, am putting you, the Confidant, within my circle of trust. I appreciate that you understand the importance of the Confidential Information I'm sharing. Because this Confidential Information is so important, I respectfully ask you to sign this Agreement and keep your promise not to disclose it.

I, _____ *(Confider's name)*, respectfully ask you, the Confidant, to keep my secret.

And I, _____ *(Confidant's name)*, agree to keep your secret, the Confidential Information, to myself and not share it with anyone unless I have your express permission.

Description of the Personal Confidential Information (the Secret to Be Kept): _____

_____

_____

(For example: A story idea; an idea for an invention; a business plan; I won the lottery; I was given a life-changing inheritance from my Great Aunt Mildred)

❑ (See Attachment 1, for "Additional Descriptions" of the Personal Confidential Information.)

The Personal Confidentiality Agreement begins: ___ / ___ /20___.

The Personal Confidentiality Agreement ends:

❑ When the Personal Confidentiality Agreement completes its function: _____

_____.

(For example: When I feel ready to tell other people; when a certain date has passed; when a certain age is reached; when all my paperwork is in order and I've talked to my attorney)

- ❑ When the Confider ends the Personal Confidentiality Agreement.
- ❑ On ___/___/20___.
- ❑ And/or _____.

2. Contact Information

The Confider Name: _____
FIRST   M.I.   LAST   RELATIONSHIP TO CONFIDANT

Address: _____
STREET   CITY   STATE   ZIP

Phone #:_____
HOME   WORK   MOBILE

E-mail: _____

The Confidant Name: _____
FIRST   M.I.   LAST   RELATIONSHIP TO CONFIDANT

Address: _____
STREET   CITY   STATE   ZIP

Phone #:_____
HOME   WORK   MOBILE

E-mail: _____

3. Communication

- ❑ The Confidant and the Confider will discuss Confidential Information only by the following means:
  - ❑ By phone. ❑ In writing. ❑ By e-mail. ❑ In person.
- ❑ The Confidant must tell the Confider immediately when the Confidential Information has been revealed:
  - ❑ By phone. ❑ In writing. ❑ By e-mail. ❑ In person.
- ❑ The Confider will alert the Confidant if and when information can be shared with others by ending this Agreement:
  - ❑ By phone. ❑ In writing. ❑ By e-mail. ❑ In person.
- ❑ And/or _____.

4. Privacy

The Confidant and the Confider agree to keep this Agreement and the Confidential Information private and secure by:

- ❑ Putting it in a safe place.
- ❑ Securing it under lock and key at home.
- ❑ Storing it in a safe deposit box.
- ❑ Other: _____.

5. If the Confidant Breaks the Promise

- ❑ The Confidant will lose the privilege of sharing in any additional Confidential Information with regard to this Agreement, and must delete or securely return any and all forms of the Confidential Information to the Confider.
- ❑ The Confider will hold the Confidant responsible for any damage occurring as a result of the failure to keep the Information confidential.
- ❑ The Confider will never share Confidential Information with the Confidant again.
- ❑ And/or _____.

6. In the Event of the Death of the Confider

- ❑ The Confidant is to refer to the Confidential Information instructions "In the Event of Death," in Attachment 2.
- ❑ The Confidant is to destroy any and all of the Confidential Information.
- ❑ The Confidant is free to release the Confidential Information.

7. Signatures

A. We agree to take A Sane Approach to an Emotional Issue™. This Personal Confidentiality Agreement reflects our understanding with regard to the Confidential Information. This Agreement replaces any previous agreements, oral or written, relating to the Confidential Information.

Location where this Personal Confidentiality Agreement is signed:

CITY	STATE

Confider: _____ ___/___/20___
PRINTED NAME   SIGNATURE   DATE

Confidant: _____ ___/___/20___
PRINTED NAME   SIGNATURE   DATE

Witness (if wanted): _____ ___/___/20___
PRINTED NAME   SIGNATURE   DATE

INSTRUCTIONS:

1. Before signing, make a copy of the filled-in Agreement with any attachments.
2. The Confider and the Confidant sign both the original and the copy.
3. The Confider and the Confidant both keep a signed copy.

B. When this Personal Confidentiality Agreement has ended, the Confider and the Confidant sign and date below on each other's Personal Confidentiality Agreement documents.

THANK YOU. THE PERSONAL CONFIDENTIALITY AGREEMENT IS NOW ENDED.

Confider's signature: _____ Date: ___/___/20___

Confidant's signature: _____ Date: ___/___/20___

Additional Descriptions

PHOTOGRAPHIC AND/OR ADDITIONAL DESCRIPTIONS

Describe the Personal Confidential Information in further detail:

_____

_____

_____

_____

_____

_____

_____

_____

_____

Attach any additional documentation:

❑ Photograph(s) of the Personal Confidential Information (initial and date).

❑ Video of the Personal Confidential Information (initial and date).

❑ Further documentation: _____

_____

_____.

❑ And/or _____.

INITIAL & DATE

The Confider's initials: _____ Date: ___/___/20____

The Confidant's initials: _____ Date: ___/___/20____

In the Event of the Confider's Death—Contact Information

For these intentions to be formally and legally recognized, they must be entered into a valid will.

The Confidant may release the Confidential Information to the person(s) named below:

Name: _____
         FIRST   M.I.   LAST   TITLE

Relationship to Confider: _____
         (For example: Attorney, brother or sister, parent, friend)

Address: _____
         STREET   CITY   STATE   ZIP

Phone #:_____
         MAIN   DIRECT   MOBILE

E-mail: _____

Name: _____
         FIRST   M.I.   LAST   TITLE

Relationship to Confider: _____
         (For example: Attorney, brother or sister, parent, friend)

Address: _____
         STREET   CITY   STATE   ZIP

Phone #:_____
         MAIN   DIRECT   MOBILE

E-mail: _____

INITIAL & DATE

The Confider's initials: _____ Date: ____/____/20____

The Confidant's initials: _____ Date: ____/____/20____

Witness' initials (if wanted): _____ Date: ____/____/20____

CHAPTER 13

Where Is Your Rent Check?

The Roommate Agreement

Sharing a place with a friend or several friends is a time-honored ritual of growing up. It is also a great way to help make ends meet or to have company in your later years. No matter how old you happen to be when you decide to cohabit, having a written agreement can smooth over the inevitable rough spots, keeping the roommate experience positive for everyone.

You can use the Roommate Agreement whether you are signing a lease agreement together or if only one of you is on the lease or is the owner of the property. If you are moving into a house owned by a friend, you may not be signing a lease at all. Still, you can complete the Roommate Agreement and lay out the ground rules and expectations for living together.

Steve and Dwayne were both looking to move into the city after college, but neither could afford the high rents on his own. A mutual friend introduced them and they decided to look for a place together. They didn't know each other very well, but they were both easygoing enough guys. This is going to work out great, they thought, when they signed the lease for a spacious two-bedroom place. They didn't stop to consider how an artist and an accountant would share living space.

The first and most obvious consideration when you decide to live together is establishing how the rent will get paid. In your agreement you will write down what the total rent is and what each person's share will be. This may go hand in hand with your discussion of who gets the bigger bedroom, the private bathroom, or the covered parking spot. You will note when and how the rent will be paid to the landlord or property owner. If someone is moving in with another person who already is leasing or owns the place, you might have an arrangement that doesn't include money.

Less obvious is that you will need to spell out how utilities—electricity, gas, water—will be paid for. Are they covered in your rent or will you be billed separately? If so, who will be handling those bills? This is a good time to discuss phone, Internet, and cable service, too. Are you in agreement about what type of service you want? If not, you may decide that one person will subscribe and have the service installed in her room only. You'll see that the agreement includes an attachment where you can write this all out, so that there isn't confusion down the line.

You'll also want to establish in advance what a roommate needs to do if she decides to move out. If your lease allows a sublease, you might write into your agreement that the remaining roommate gets to approve the replacement for the one who's leaving. You'll also specify how the deposit and other expenses will be carried over.

The fun part of living with someone is in the living together. This can also be the tough part. You will get to know someone's personal habits and routines in an intimate way—whether you want to or not. This is where an agreement is especially helpful. Once you lay out each person's household responsibilities—cooking, cleaning, security—and their preferences—pets, parties, overnight guests—you will be leaving a lot less to interpretation. The agreement allows you to go into as little or as much detail as you need to be comfortable. You will consider issues such as smoking, drinking, and substance use. When you talk through the agreement, you may find out that your new roommate's boyfriend is a smoker. Together you can establish that he can smoke only on the balcony. Or you may discover that your cat isn't universally loved and you will have to figure out a way to keep him out of your roommate's bedroom. You will talk about how each of you is to protect your property and who else, if anyone, is allowed to have a key to the home or apartment.

Edna and Flo were lifelong friends who decided to take an apartment together after they were both widowed. Edna's son, Frank, lived nearby and that gave comfort to both women. Flo didn't realize though that Edna had given Frank a key to the apartment "just in case." Unfortunately, Frank developed the habit of coming over to check-in without warning. When Flo came out of the bathroom in her towel one morning to find Frank standing there, it was the last straw. But now she wasn't sure how to tell Edna that Frank wasn't welcome to let himself in.

The Roommate Agreement will ask roommates to consider any special courtesies they would like observed. If you are a student, you may want to specify that the living space needs to be quiet on weeknights to allow you to study. If you work nights, you may need to write down that during your daytime sleeping hours you don't want guests visiting.

Since good communication is at the heart of any positive relationship, your agreement will help you set up a regular forum for talking. A regularly scheduled meeting to discuss how things are working can keep minor issues from becoming major problems. If problems should arise, your agreement will outline your options for dealing with them. Consequences might include financial penalties, for instance, if damage is done to the apartment and you are required to pay for repairs, or even having to leave the shared residence.

Courtesy and respect must always be practiced when you are living under the same roof. Life can be unbearable when there is tension in your home environment. Even if you take the time to create the best written agreement in the world, you and your roommate will need to be considerate of each other and willing to adapt to changing needs and situations. When you sign, you are committing to do just that.

FAMILY & FRIENDS AGREEMENT

Roommate Agreement

PAPER HANDSHAKE · PRINTED PROMISE · PUBLISHED COMMITMENT

As Roommates, we are making this Agreement because:

Roommate A's reasons: _____

_____

_____

Roommate B's reasons: _____

_____

_____

(For example: To share rent and expenses; to have companionship; to live with my best friend; to try out a new area of town or city)

1. The Promise

We, Roommate A and Roommate B, hereby agree to share this apartment/house/condo (the Shared Residence). This document serves as an Agreement between both of us in order to avoid any misunderstandings or difficulties that may arise due to sharing a living space.

I, _____ (Roommate A's name), agree to share a residence with
(PRINT NAME)

_____ (Roommate B's name), at: _____
(PRINT NAME)

_____
(ADDRESS OF THE SHARED RESIDENCE)

The Shared Residence is:

❑ An apartment/house/condo that will be leased by ❑ Roommate A and/or ❑ Roommate B.

❑ An apartment/house/condo already owned or occupied by ❑ Roommate A or ❑ Roommate B.

❑ And/or _____.

The Shared Residence begins on ___/___/20___

❑ And/or _____.

The Shared Residence ends on ___/___/20___

❑ And/or _____.

Rent will be paid:

❑ By both Roommate A and Roommate B to the Landlord.

❑ By Roommate _____ to Roommate _____ for the Shared Residence already owned or occupied by Roommate _____.

❑ And/or _____.

2. Contact Information

Roommate A Name: _____
                                FIRST   M.I.   LAST

Address: _____
              STREET   CITY   STATE   ZIP

Phone #:_____
            HOME   WORK   MOBILE

E-mail: _____

Roommate B Name: _____
                                  FIRST   M.I.   LAST

Address: _____
              STREET   CITY   STATE   ZIP

Phone #:_____
            HOME   WORK   MOBILE

E-mail: _____

The Landlord: _____
                      FIRST   M.I.   LAST   TITLE

Address: _____
              STREET   CITY   STATE   ZIP

Phone #:_____
            HOME   WORK   MOBILE

E-mail: _____

3. Finances and Shared Expenses

Rent payments:

❏ Roommate ____ will pay to Roommate _____ $_____ on the _____ day of each _____ for Rent if the Shared Residence is owned or occupied by the other Roommate.

❏ Roommate A will pay $_____ and Roommate B will pay $ _____ to the Landlord on the _____ day of each _____ for Rent.

❏ See Schedule A, "Renter's Payment Plan in Place of Cash Payment."

❏ And/or _____.

Monies due at lease signing:

❏ See Schedule B, "Deposit and Utilities."

Utilities (water, cable, electric, phone, and other):

❑ Utilities are included in Rent.

❑ See Schedule B, "Deposit and Utilities."

Shared expenses (groceries, cleaning supplies, etc.)

❑ See Schedule C, "Shared Expenses."

Renter's insurance:

❑ Roommates maintain Renter's Insurance.

❑ See Schedule C, "Shared Expenses."

Roommate leaves before lease is up (if rental lease allows):

❑ Leaving Roommate must continue to pay Rent until the end of the lease or find a suitable replacement roommate agreeable to the remaining Roommate.

❑ And/or _____.

4. Living Space (Living and Parking)

❑ Roommate A and Roommate B equally share space in the apartment/house/condo.

❑ Roommate A defines his/her space as follows: _____

_____

❑ Roommate B defines his/her space as follows: _____

_____

❑ Roommate A and Roommate B define common shared areas as follows: _____

_____

❑ And/or _____.

5. Responsibilities and Policies

Household Responsibilities:

Roommates agree to:

❑ Clean up after themselves and their guest(s) and pet(s) (if allowed).

❑ Do their own grocery shopping and food preparation.

❑ Do their own laundry and ironing.

❑ Keep common spaces clean and free of clutter.

❑ Contribute to shared household responsibilities (see Schedule D, "Shared Household Responsibilities").

❑ And/or _____.

Guest(s) and Overnight Guest(s):

❑ No more than _____ guests in the house at any given time.

❑ No overnight guests at any time.

❑ No stranger(s) as overnight guest(s).

❑ No overnight guests the other Roommate feels unsafe or uncomfortable having overnight.

❑ Always check with Roommate _____ day(s) in advance if entertaining more than _____ (number of) guests to make sure it works with the other Roommate's schedule.

- ❑ Always check with Roommate ____ day(s) or ____ hour(s) in advance of having an overnight guest to make sure that it works with the other Roommate's schedule.
- ❑ A Roommate may not allow another person to move into the residence with him/her. A person is considered to have moved in if he/she stays more than ____ consecutive nights.
- ❑ All guests respect the same Household Policies (below).
- ❑ And/or _____.

Pets:

- ❑ Pet(s) is/are allowed and the pet owner is responsible to clean, feed, care for, and supervise his/her pet(s).
- ❑ Non-owning pet Roommate is not responsible for anything that happens to pet owner's pet while residing in the Shared Residence.
- ❑ If the pet(s) becomes an issue it/they have to go.
- ❑ No pets allowed.
- ❑ And/or _____.

Household Policies:

- ❑ No smoking in the house.
- ❑ Respect each other's personal space within the Shared Residence and agree not to enter the other's private space without knocking or without permission.
- ❑ No drug use will be tolerated.
- ❑ Alcohol may be consumed in moderation.
- ❑ For safety purposes, Roommates will keep each other informed of their whereabouts in case of an emergency.
- ❑ If one Roommate will be coming home late or not coming home at all, he/she will call and let the other Roommate know, regardless of the hour.
- ❑ Each Roommate will keep the Shared Residence locked at all times.
- ❑ No keys to the Shared Residence will be given to anyone else; only Roommate A and Roommate B will have keys to the Shared Residence.
- ❑ Roommate will rekey and pay for the new lock(s) to the Shared Residence if his/her key to that lock(s) is lost.
- ❑ Roommates will alert each other in a timely manner ____ week(s) prior if they foresee being late with a Rent or a Utility payment.
- ❑ And/or _____.

6. Communication

Messages:

- ❑ Roommates A and B will take messages for one another and place those messages promptly in the following place: _____
- ❑ Roommates A and B will not take messages for one another.
- ❑ And/or _____.

Meetings:

- ❑ Roommates A and B will meet regularly to discuss how the shared living arrangements are working out. That date will be the _____(day) of each _____(month/week).
- ❑ And/or _____.

Emergency Roommate Contacts:

- ❑ Complete Attachment, titled "Emergency Contacts."

7. Additional Roommate Considerations

Every situation is unique; take a moment to add additional considerations.

Roommate A adds the following considerations:

- ❑ _____
- ❑ _____
- ❑ _____

Roommate B adds the following considerations:

- ❑ _____
- ❑ _____
- ❑ _____

8. If the Promise Is Broken

- ❑ A Roommate who doesn't pay Rent and/or Utility bills must pay any costs associated with not paying such as a late fee.
- ❑ A Roommate who leaves before the lease expires pays for costs associated with leaving early or

    _____

- ❑ A Roommate who is responsible for damages to the Shared Residence, including damage done by her/his guest(s) or pet(s), is responsible for paying the costs of those damages, including resulting fines or money withheld by the Landlord from the security deposit both Roommates paid at lease signing or

    _____

- ❑ A Roommate who is responsible for damaging the other Roommate's personal property, including damage done by her/his guest(s) or pet(s), is responsible for the costs of replacing the property or repaiting it to as good as its previous condition _____
- ❑ A Roommate will receive a verbal reminder of the specific term(s) he/she is not honoring.
- ❑ A Roommate will be shown the specific terms, on our signed Agreement, which he/she is not honoring.
- ❑ And/or _____.

9. Signatures

- **A.** We agree to take A Sane Approach to an Emotional Issue™. This Roommate Agreement reflects our understanding of the intentions with regard to the Shared Residence. This Agreement replaces any previous agreements, oral or written, relating to their Shared Residence.

Location where this Roommate Agreement is signed:

_____
CITY   STATE

Roommate A: _____ ___/___/20___
                    PRINTED NAME   SIGNATURE   DATE

Roommate B: _____ ___/___/20___
                    PRINTED NAME   SIGNATURE   DATE

INSTRUCTIONS:

1. Before signing, make a copy of the filled-in Agreement with any schedules or attachments.

2. Roommate A and Roommate B sign both the original, and the copy.

3. Roommate A and Roommate B both keep a signed copy.

B. When the Roommate Agreement has ended, Roommate A and Roommate B sign and date below on both Agreement documents—Roommate A's document, and Roommate B's document.

THANK YOU. THIS ROOMMATE AGREEMENT IS NOW ENDED

Roommate A's Signature:_____ Date: ___/___/20___

Roommate B's Signature:_____ Date: ___/___/20___

Renter's Payment Plan in Place of Cash Payment

Renter's name: _____

Phone number: _____

E-mail address: _____

RENTER'S PAYMENT SCHEDULE

PAYMENT	DESCRIPTION OF THE WORK	START DATE (MONTH/DAY/YEAR)	COMPLETED (MONTH/DAY/YEAR)	TOTAL $ AMOUNT WORK REPRESENTS	ACKNOWLEDGE*
1					
2					
3					
4					
5					
6					
7					
8					
9					
10					
11					
12					
13					
14					
15					
16					
17					
18					
19					
20					

*All work should be acknowledged with signature or initials of Roommate.

Deposit and Utilities

MONIES DUE AT LEASE SIGNING

MONIES DUE	ROOMMATE A	ROOMMATE B
First month's Rent		
Last month's Rent		
Security deposit		
Pet deposit		
And		
TOTAL DUE:		

MONIES DUE TO START UTILITIES

UTILITY TYPE	TOTAL $ TO GET UTILITY TURNED ON	A'S NAME	B'S NAME	IN BOTH NAMES	A PAYS $	B PAYS $
Phone landline						
Internet						
TV						
Gas						
Electric						
Water						
Trash						
TOTAL DUE:						

Shared Expenses

ONGOING UTILITY PAYMENTS

UTILITY TYPE	TOTAL $ TO PAY TO UTILITY CO.	A PAYS UTILITY CO.	B PAYS UTILITY CO.	BOTH PAY UTILITY CO.	A PAYS % OF UTILITY	B PAYS % OF UTILITY
Phone landline						
Internet						
TV						
Gas						
Electric						
Water						
Trash						
TOTAL DUE:						

ADDITIONAL SHARED EXPENSES

(Examples are in italics.)

EXPENSE TYPE	COST	A PAYS % OF COST	B PAYS % OF COST
Cleaning Supplies	*$$$*	*50%*	*50%*
Shared Groceries	*$$$*	*25%*	*75%*
Renter's Insurance			

INITIAL & DATE

Roommate A's Initials: _____ Date: ____/____/20____

Roommate B's Initials: _____ Date: ____/____/20____

Shared Household Responsibilities

Define details and Roommate commitment. (Examples are in italics.)

COMMON AREAS	DAILY	WEEKLY	MONTHLY	AS NEEDED	DETERMINE RESPONSIBILITIES FOR EACH: ROOMMATE A AND/OR ROOMMATE B
Living room					
Vacuum		X			*Roommates alternate every other week*
Dust					
Kitchen					
Empty dishwasher				X	*Roommate B*
Take out garbage					
Community Bathroom					
Clean sink					

(continued)

COMMON AREAS	DAILY	WEEKLY	MONTHLY	AS NEEDED	DETERMINE RESPONSIBILITIES FOR EACH: ROOMMATE A AND/OR ROOMMATE B
Yard					
Cooking/Groceries					
Other					

INITIAL & DATE

Roommate A's Initials: _____ Date: ___/___/20___

Roommate B's Initials: _____ Date: ___/___/20___

ROOMMATES AGREEMENT, ATTACHMENT

EMERGENCY CONTACTS

EMERGENCY CONTACT FOR ROOMMATE A

Name: _____
      FIRST   LAST   RELATIONSHIP TO ROOMMATE A

Address: _____
      STREET   CITY   STATE   ZIP

Phone #:_____
      HOME   WORK   MOBILE

E-mail: _____

EMERGENCY CONTACT FOR ROOMMATE B

Name: _____
      FIRST   LAST   RELATIONSHIP TO ROOMMATE B

Address: _____
      STREET   CITY   STATE   ZIP

Phone #:_____
      HOME   WORK   MOBILE

E-mail: _____

CHAPTER 14

Do It Yourself

Blank Agreement for Any Arrangement

In this book we put together agreements that we thought would be of the greatest use to the most people. We addressed common circumstances and typical problems people have. However, you may have an unusual situation that would benefit from the Sane Approach, one that we can't anticipate because it's specific to you. That's why we prepared a blank agreement that can serve as a form for creating your own.

For instance, you and a friend might be taking turns looking after each other's children and you might want to make sure you agree on things like who will pay for what and how the children will be cared for. Is the person who has them responsible for providing food or are the children supposed to bring their own lunch and/or snacks? What kind of safety precautions do you expect in your absence? How will the kids be disciplined? Are there medical issues you want to address? What happens if one of you gets sick?

This arrangement, like many other situations, might benefit from a written agreement. Often when people share things (like a car or child care) parameters must be set. Or you might want to enter into an agreement if you are going to share a task like carpooling or hosting an event. Even if you want to do something as simple as making sure that everyone knows a certain item was a gift and not a loan, you could put that in writing. This blank form should help you create something on your own, specific to what you need.

The form starts with a simple statement summarizing what the agreement is about and whom the agreement is between. For example, with the situation described above you might say: "This is an agreement regarding mutual babysitting services." Then you would fill in the blanks for the names of the people involved. Other examples of good ways to fill in that first blank are:

This is an agreement regarding:

- The use of a shared driveway

- The use of shared lawn equipment

- A gift

- School carpooling

- Susan's bridal shower

Once you have identified the nature of the agreement and the parties involved, you should set down the goals of each party to make sure you understand what each person is anticipating. So, for instance, in the babysitting scenario, Pam's goal might be to have consistent after-school care for her children while Amy might be doing it because she wants company for her only child or needs some extra money. Knowing why people want to do certain things is crucial when it comes to deciding how they will be done.

Once you have filled out the reasons for the agreement, you must decide exactly what the promise is. What are you really agreeing to do? To do this, you must spell out each party's obligations specifically and thoroughly. Here are some examples of ways to phrase the promise:

Dion and Leo agree to buy a snowblower together. They will share the cost of the snowblower and any related costs equally. It will be stored in Dion's garage.

Ann, Connie, and Sue agree to plan and pay for Erica's baby shower. We agree to split the cost of the shower in thirds. The entire shower will cost approximately $750. The shower will be held at Ann's house, Connie will order the food, and Sue will address and mail the invitations.

Next you have to decide how you will communicate. Who is supposed to contact whom and how? What information would you like to make sure gets conveyed? For example, in the above situations you might want to say:

When it snows, Dion will call to consult with Leo on who will use the blower first or offer to clear both properties in exchange for Leo clearing both properties during the next storm. Both men agree to call each other if the snowblower needs gas or repair.

We agree to consult with one another before we make any purchases over $25. We agree to make the decisions regarding the invitations, food, and decorations together.

You have to consider if there is anything you want to make sure is done in a certain way. In the Special Circumstances or Requirements section you would lay out any specifics. You might want to spell out who pays for what in the shower scenario, or you might want to specify who will set up and clean up. If you are planning to offer babysitting services, you might want to specify how you will handle paying for food and diapers and what methods of discipline are acceptable. With respect to car sharing, you might want to spell out what happens if the car breaks down or gets towed.

Of course, as always, you have to consider what will happen if one party does not do what he agreed to do. With Dion and Leo's agreement, if Leo doesn't pay for his share of the gas, he will lose his use of the snowblower. With the shared baby shower, the women may want to agree that if anyone buys something without consulting the others, she will be responsible for the cost of that item, but must still share equally in the cost of everything else.

Depending on the kind of agreement you are entering into, filling out all the parts of the document may not be necessary. If you are in a babysitting arrangement, for example, you won't need to use the In the Event of Death section. Fill out those sections that are appropriate and feel free to add new parts, if necessary. You can also use extra paper to write out additional conditions and requirements, if you have to. The most important parts to include are the names of the people involved, what both sides are promising, and the signatures.

Use this blank agreement as a guide. Instead of just saying, "Okay, sure" or "That sounds like a good idea," you can put your thoughts in writing and have something to refer to when memories fade or circumstances change.

Blank Agreement for Any Arrangement

PAPER HANDSHAKE · PRINTED PROMISE · PUBLISHED COMMITMENT

Person A and Person B are making this agreement because . . .

Person A's reason(s): _____

_____

Person B's reason(s): _____

_____

1. The Promise

I/we promise to: _____

_____

_____

_____

I/we, _____ (Person A's name), agree _____

_____.

And I/we, _____ (Person B's name), also agree _____

_____.

2. Contact Information

Person A, Name: _____
           FIRST   M.I.   LAST   RELATIONSHIP TO PERSON B

Address: _____
      STREET   CITY   STATE   ZIP

Phone #:_____
      HOME   WORK   MOBILE

E-mail: _____

Person B, Name: _____
           FIRST   M.I.   LAST   RELATIONSHIP TO PERSON A

Address: _____
      STREET   CITY   STATE   ZIP

Phone #:_____
      HOME   WORK   MOBILE

E-mail: _____

3. Communication

Determine how to keep each other informed:

_____
_____
_____
_____

❏   See Schedule A for additional details.

4. Special Circumstances or Requirements

Explain any specific requirements or special circumstances:

_____
_____
_____
_____

❏   See Schedule A for additional details.

5. If the Promise Is Broken . . .

Although we do not anticipate any problem, we do think it is wise to include consequences in our Agreement, just in case a problem arises or the promise is broken.

_____
_____
_____
_____

6. In the Event of the Death of Person A or Person B

For these intentions to be formally and legally recognized, they must be entered into a valid will.

Person A and Person B may indicate below what they each intend to do with respect to this Agreement in the event of either's death.

_____
_____
_____
_____

❏   See Attachment 1, "In the Event of the Death . . ." for more detailed information.

7. Signatures

A. We agree to take A Sane Approach to an Emotional Issue™. This Agreement reflects our understanding of the intentions with regard to _____

Location where this Agreement is signed: _____
                                                          CITY   STATE

Person A: _____ ____/____ /20____
                      SIGNATURE   PRINTED NAME   DATE

Person B: _____ ____/____ /20____
                      SIGNATURE   PRINTED NAME   DATE

Witness (if wanted): _____ ____/____ /20____
                                SIGNATURE   PRINTED NAME   DATE

INSTRUCTIONS:

1. Before signing, make a copy of the filled-in Agreement with schedule or attachment.

2. Persons A and B both sign the original and the copy.

3. Persons A and B both keep a signed copy.

B. When this Agreement has ended, Person A and Person B sign and date below on both documents—Person A's document, and Person B's document.

THANK YOU. THE AGREEMENT IS NOW ENDED

Person A's signature: _____ Date: ____/____/20 ____

Person B's signature: _____ Date: ____/____/20 ____

BLANK AGREEMENT FOR ANY ARRANGEMENT, SCHEDULE A

Please fill in the details of the Agreement to ensure that everyone understands the commitment/arrangement.

PERSON A	PERSON B	

INITIAL & DATE

Person A's initials: _____ Date: ____/____/20____

Person B's initials: _____ Date: ____/____/20____

In the Event of the Death of Person A or Person B

Decide what should happen in the event of Person A's death.

_____

_____

_____

Decide what should happen in the event of Person B's death.

_____

_____

_____

For these intentions to be formally and legally recognized, they must be entered into a valid will.

PERSON A'S DESIGNATED REPRESENTATIVE'S CONTACT INFORMATION

Name: _____
     FIRST   M.I.   LAST   TITLE

Address: _____
     STREET   CITY   STATE   ZIP

Phone #:_____
     HOME   WORK   MOBILE

E-mail: _____

PERSON B'S DESIGNATED REPRESENTATIVE'S CONTACT INFORMATION

Name: _____
     FIRST   M.I.   LAST   TITLE

Address: _____
     STREET   CITY   STATE   ZIP

Phone #:_____
     HOME   WORK   MOBILE

E-mail: _____

INITIAL & DATE

Person A's initials: _____ Date: ___/___/20____

Person B's initials: _____ Date: ___/___/20____

Witness's initials (if wanted): _____ Date: ___/___/20____

INDEX

A

Adult child moving back home.
    See Temporary residence
    (grown child returns home)
Amounts, clarifying, 13–14
Arbitration, 22
Asking questions, 17
Attachments. *See Agreements Index*;
    Schedules and attachments
Attorney letter, 22

B

Basic information, 12
Benefits of written agreements
    avoiding misunderstandings, 8,
        11–12
    considering consequences of
        decision, 7–8
    explaining. *See* Presenting idea
        of agreements
    revealing level of commitment,
        7–8
Blank agreement
    forms, *immediately after page 153*
    forms overview, 151–152
    possible uses for, 151
    using, 151–153
Borrowing money. *See* Lending/
    borrowing money

C

Caring for aging parents, 77–90
    agreement, *follows page 79*
    avoiding misunderstandings,
        11–12
    blueprint for conversation
        about, 77–78
    decision-making process, 79
    examples illustrating need for
        agreement, 77, 78, 79

financial considerations, 79
    ill or incapacitated parent, 78
    keeping lines of communication
        open, 79
    rationale for written agreement,
        77–79
Changes to agreement
    discussing, 19
    drifting from agreement and,
        19–20
    new attachments/adjusted
        schedules, 19
    preparing for, 16
    renegotiation, 19
Commitment, discerning level of,
    7–8
Confidentiality. *See* Personal
    confidentiality
Contact information, 12
Copying agreement, 17

D

Dates
    being specific with periods and,
        13
    of signing agreement, 12
Death, planning for possibility of, 16
Deciding for agreements. *See*
    Benefits of written
    agreements; Presenting idea
    of agreements
Defaulting on agreements
    handling. *See* Enforcing
        agreements
    planning for, 16
Detail
    accurately identifying property,
        14
    clarity of amounts and values,
        13–14

comfort levels with, 9–10
    specific periods and dates, 13
    thoroughness of agreement,
        12–13
    of triggering events, 13
Dispute resolution. *See* Enforcing
    agreements
Driving agreement. *See* Safe
    driving agreement

E

Enforcing agreements, 19–23
    arbitration, 22
    attorney letter, 22
    easy way, 20–21
    formal dispute resolution, 21–22
    letters for, 20–21, 22
    mediation, 22
    renegotiation and, 19
    simple communication first, 20
    Small Claims Court, 19, 22–23
Exclusions, 15

F

Formal dispute resolution, 21–22

H

How actions are carried out,
    delineating, 14–15

L

Lending/borrowing money, 27–38
    agreement, *follows page 29*
    amounts, interest rates, tax
        implications, 28–29
    deciding for/against, 27–28
    examples illustrating need for
        agreement, 2–3, 27–28, 29
    Failure to Pay section, 29
    level of detail in, 29

Lending/borrowing money *(continued)*
    possible complications/
      consequences, 28
    rationale for written agreement,
      9, 27–29
    reasons for, 29
    repayment terms, 29
Lending personal property, 39–47
    agreement, *follows page 41*
    caring for item by borrower, 41
    condition of property, 39–40
    conditions/limitations on use,
      40, 41
    description of property, 40
    examples illustrating need for
      agreement, 2, 40, 41
    goals for lender and borrower, 40
    rationale for written agreement,
      39–41
    risk of, 41
    time frame for loan, 40
Lending vacation home, 115–125
    agreement, *follows page 117*
    condition of property and, 117
    delineating property and
      responsibilities, 116–117
    examples illustrating need for
      agreement, 7–8, 115, 116, 117
    fees and expense considerations,
      116
    limitations on use, 117
    rationale for written agreement,
      115–117
    security issues, 117
Letters, for enforcing agreements
    attorney writing, 22
    sample letters, 21
    writing, 20–21
Listening
    explaining reason for
      agreement and, 8–9
    understanding needs of both
      parties and, 8, 9

M
Mediation, 22
Misunderstandings
    avoiding misrepresentations
      as, 12

honest, avoiding, 8, 11–12
Money, lending. *See* Lending/
    borrowing money

N
Names of parties involved, 12

P
Parents, caring for. *See* Caring for
    aging parents
Personal confidentiality, 127–133
    agreement, *follows page 128*
    examples illustrating need for
      agreement, 127, 128
    goals in sharing information,
      128
    identifying confidential
      information, 128
    means of passing information,
      128
    rationale for written agreement,
      127–128
    remedies for default, 128
    security issues, 128
    when confidential information
      can be revealed, 128
Personal property. *See* Lending
    personal property
Pet parenting. *See* Shared pet/pet
    parenting
Presenting idea of agreements.
    See also specific types of
    agreements
    avoiding future
      misunderstandings and, 8
    considering consequences of
      decision and, 7–8
    phrases to use, 8–9
Property
    identifying accurately, 14
    lending. *See* Lending personal
      property
    noting condition of, 14
Putting things in writing
    examples illustrating value of,
      1–3
    key reason for, 3
    levels of detail in, 9–10
    phrases to use supporting, 8–9

resistance to, 8. *See also*
    Presenting idea of
    agreements

Q
Questions, asking, 17

R
Reading agreements aloud, 17
Rent issues. *See* Roommate
    agreement; Temporary
    residence (grown child
    returns home)
Roommate agreement, 135–150
    agreement, *follows page 137*
    communication ground rules,
      137
    delineating responsibilities, 136
    establishing rent payment
      method, 135–136
    examples illustrating need for
      agreement, 135, 136
    if one person moves out, 136
    rationale for, 135–137
    special courtesies, 136
    sublease terms, 136
    utility expenses, 136

S
Safe driving agreement, 91–101
    agreement, *follows page 93*
    communication ground rules,
      92
    delineating/enforcing rules, 93
    examples illustrating need for,
      91–92, 93
    one-sided nature of, 92
    overview, 92–93
    rationale for written agreement,
      91–93
    reviewing with teen, 92
Sane Approach to an Emotional
    Issue
    justifying agreement and.
      See Benefits of written
      agreements; Presenting idea
      of agreements
    origins of, 1–4
Schedules and attachments

defined, 14
making changes later, 19
using when necessary, 14
Shared parenting for separated/
divorced parents, 63–75
agreement, *follows page 65*
communication ground rules,
64
compromises in, 64
examples illustrating need for
agreement, 63, 64
putting children first, 63
rationale for written agreement,
63–65
Shared pet/pet parenting, 103–113
agreement, *follows page 106*
delineating responsibilities, 105
duration of agreement, 105–106
examples illustrating need for
agreement, 104, 105
identifying pet in agreement,
104–105
life span of pet and, 104–106
parent using agreement with
child, 105
pre-agreement considerations,
103–104
rationale for written agreement,
103–106
Signing agreements
asking questions before, 17
having third party read before,
17
making copies after, 17
reading aloud before, 17
sleeping on before, 17
things to do after, 17–18
things to do before, 17
tracking activities after, 17
Sleeping on proposed agreement,
17
Small Claims Court
avoiding if possible, 19

cases handled by, 22–23
dollar range handled by, 22–23
finding additional information
on, 23
function of, 22

T
Temporary residence (grown child
returns home)
agreement, *follows page 53*
changes to agreement, 53
consequences of failing to
comply with agreement, 53
examples illustrating need
for agreement, 3, 9–10, 49,
50–51, 52
guest provisions, 52
household/personal expenses
and, 51–52
length of stay, 51
partying and social behaviors,
52
personal quirks and, 52–53
rationale for written agreement,
49–53
rent considerations, 51, 52
scope of agreement, 51–53
use of family car and, 52
Third party, reading agreement, 17
Thoroughness of agreement, 12–13
Tracking things
agreeing on methods of, 15
following through on, 17
Triggering events
delineating clearly, 13
when they don't happen, 16

U
Unexpected events
changes to agreement, 16
death, 16
one side doesn't follow through,
16

preparing for, 16
triggering events don't happen,
16

V
Vacation home use. See Lending
vacation home
Values, clarifying, 13–14

W
Writing agreements, 11–18. *See also
Agreements Index; specific
types of agreements*
accurately identifying property,
14
agreeing on how to track
things, 15
allowing for changes, 16
amounts and values, 13–14
avoiding dishonest
misunderstandings by, 12
avoiding honest
misunderstandings by,
11–12
basic information, 12
death contingencies and, 16
delineating dispute resolution,
16
excluding things, 15
filling in blanks, 12–16
including things, 15
noting condition of property, 14
preparing for unexpected, 16
saying *what* and *how*, 14–15
signing after. *See* Signing
agreements
specific periods and dates in, 13
thoroughness in, 12–13
triggering events, 13, 16
using schedules or attachments
as necessary, 14

Blank Agreement for Any
 Arrangement (follows page
 153)
 Agreement, i–iii
 Attachment 1: In the Event of
 the Death of Person A or
 Person B, v
 Schedule A, iv

Caring for Our Aging Parents
 Agreement (follows page79)
 Agreement, i–v
 Attachment 1: Additional
 Siblings 5 through 7 Contact
 Information, ix
 Schedule A: Sharing
 Responsibilities, vi
 Schedule B: Rest for the
 Primary Caregiver and
 Visiting, vii
 Schedule C: Our Parent(s)'
 Expenses, viii

Lending Personal Property
 Agreement (follows page 41)
 Agreement, i–iii
 Attachment 1: Photographic
 Documentation Record, iv
 Attachment 2: In the Event of
 the Death of the Lender or
 Borrower, v

Lending Your Vacation Home
 Agreement (follows page
 117)
 Agreement, i–iv
 Attachment 1: Photographic
 Documentation Record, vi
 Attachment 2: Vacation Home
 Favorite Activities, vii
 Schedule A: Bartered Rent
 Payment in Place of
 Monetary Rent Payment, v

Lend Money Agreement (follows
 page 29)
 Agreement, i–iv
 Attachment 1: In the Event of
 the Death of the Lender or
 the Borrower, viii
 Schedule A: Loan Repayment
 Plan and Record, v
 Schedule B: Loan Repayment
 Plan—In Place of Cash
 Payment, vi
 Schedule C: Repayment for
 Loan with Interest, vii

Personal Confidentiality
 Agreement (follows page
 128)
 Agreement, i–iii
 Attachment 1: Additional
 Descriptions, iv
 Attachment 2: In the Event
 of the Confider's Death—
 Contact Information, v

Roommate Agreement (follows
 page 137)
 Agreement, i–vi
 Attachment: Emergency
 Contacts, xii
 Schedule A: Renter's Payment
 Plan in Place of Cash
 Payment, vii
 Schedule B: Depoists and
 Utilities, viii
 Schedule C: Shared Expenses, ix
 Schedule D: Shared Household
 Responsibilities, x–xi

Safe Driving Parent–Teen Driver
 Agreement (follows page 93)
 Agreement, i–v
 Attachment 1: In Case of
 Accident, vi–vii

Shared Parenting for Separated/
 Divorced Parents
 Agreement (follows page 65)
 Agreement, i–iv
 Attachment 1: Emergency
 Contact List, ix
 Schedule A: Contact and
 Visitation—Detailed
 Choices, v
 Schedule B: Vacation and
 Holiday Schedule: Detailed
 Choices, vi
 Schedule C: Decision Making:
 Our Children's Day-to-Day
 Rules and Routines, vii
 Schedule D: Decision Making:
 Major Parenting Decisions,
 viii

Shared Pet/Pet Parenting
 Agreement (follows page
 106)
 Agreement, i–iv
 Attachment 1: Pet Identification
 Record, vi
 Attachment 2: In the Event of
 the Death of the Sole Owner
 Pet Parent, vii
 Schedule A: Pet Care
 Responsibilities and
 Expenses, v

Temporary Residence/Grown
 Child Returns Home
 Agreement (follows page 53)
 Agreement, i–vi
 Schedule A: Household
 Responsibilities, vii

ABOUT THE AUTHORS

DEBORAH HUTCHISON is the cofounder and CEO of Panther Productions Inc., a company specializing in film, publishing, and product design. Shortly after graduating from William Woods University (where she still sits as a trustee) with a degree in secondary education, a friend dared Hutchison to apply to be an extra on the set of the now-legendary movie, *The Blues Brothers*. Her application was accepted, and she quickly fell in love with the movie business, leading her to form the Rosen-Knutsen Casting Company. Rosen-Knutsen rapidly rose to become one of the most successful film and television casting companies in Chicago. In 1984, Hutchison was voted into the Director's Guild of America—one of the first females to receive this honor in Chicago.

Hutchison went on to found Panther Productions with her husband and technical producer, Hall Hutchison. Panther Productions has been engaged by NBC, ABC, and Columbia Pictures to provide cutting-edge visual services.

As a result of challenging issues she experienced with her first husband, Hutchison created the Bill Your Ex system, a.k.a. BYX—a popular tool to collect court-ordered support payments from spouses. For this original product design, she was awarded the 1990 Lammie Award for "Best New Product in a Law-Related Field." BYX became nationally noted throughout the legal circuit, and she appeared in magazine features and on syndicated talk and radio shows.

Currently Deborah is seeking to empower girls and women through Gutsy Gals Inspire Me™, an initiative that will profile extraordinary historical women from throughout the world who changed the course of history. Promoting the value of persistence and encouraging a life of possibility, Hutchison is creating a series of "Gutsy Gals" films, books and merchandise tie-ins. Learn more by visiting http://www.gutsygalsinspireme.com.

LYNN TOLER, originally from Columbus, Ohio, earned her undergraduate degree in English and American literature from Harvard and her Juris Doctorate from the University of Pennsylvania Law School. As a litigator, Toler tried cases at all levels, from Municipal to Common Pleas to Federal Court. Between 1986 and 1994, she also served as an arbitrator in Cuyahoga County's Common Pleas Court. In 1994, she was elected administrative judge in Cleveland Heights Municipal Court, and during her eight-year tenure she oversaw hundreds of small claims, domestic violence, assault, and stalking cases. As a municipal judge, Toler witnessed a lot of failed friendships and fractured families that never had to be—if only the parties had just "put it in writing."

While a sitting judge, Toler was the recipient of the 2002 Humanitarian Award by the Cleveland, Ohio, Domestic Violence Center. After retiring from the bench in 2001, she developed law courses and served as an adjunct professor at Ursuline College. Toler also authored *My Mother's Rules: A Practical Guide to Becoming an Emotional Genius,* a book about emotional control—what it is and how to find it.

Since 2006, Toler has been the host of *Divorce Court,* a nationally syndicated, relationship-oriented court show produced by Twentieth Century Television. She also the hosted the prime-time television show *Decision House* in 2007–2008 and is currently a bimonthly contributor to *News and Notes* on National Public Radio. Toler is a frequent guest on national television, sharing her expertise on a variety of issues on shows such as *The O'Reilly Factor, Montell Williams, The Tyra Banks Show, Larry King Live,* and *The Dr. Phil Show.* Recently, she began a featured column in *Divorce Magazine,* titled "Ask Judge Lynn." In 2009 Judge Lynn was awarded The National Voice of Freedom Award by the Philadelphia Martin Luther King, Jr. Association for Nonviolence. Toler routinely speaks on a variety of topics all over the country and maintains a Web site dedicated to emotional education at http://www.judgelynn.com.